BEST OF ENGLAND

REMARKABLE TRAVEL GUIDES

Welcome to Best of England and thank you for selecting one of our travel guides.

We are a small, independent publisher aiming to make the best books that we can to promote our amazing country, England. We strive to champion other small, innovative and creative businesses who are as passionate about what they are doing as we are. We think that the best way to do this is to use our photography to make the most beautiful, honest and useful books that we can.

We visited and photographed each of the recommendations featured within this guide. No business in this guide paid to be featured and we turned up unannounced, so that we would experience each one as you would.

We think that it is important for our environment to print our books in England and with FSC certified paper from responsible sources, which is why our books are a little bit more expensive than some others.

We hope to make this guide bigger and better each year. Please let me know if you have a recommendation which you feel should be included and we will do our best to feature it in the next edition. I have included my personal email below.

If you like what we are doing, please tell your friends about us. There is nothing better than word-of-mouth and it would mean a lot to us and the businesses that we represent in the books. If you give them the code "welcome" they can get 15% off their first purchase from our website (feel free to use it yourself).

I hope that you are pleased with your purchase when it arrives. If your order doesn't arrive on time or in perfect condition, please let me know and I will look into it for you.

Happy travels!

Simon Ridgwell
Editor | Best of England
simon@bestofengland.com

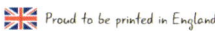 Proud to be printed in England

BEST OF ENGLAND

PLACES TO VISIT

YORKSHIRE

Beverley

PLACES TO VISIT | BEVERLEY | HU17 0AB

Beverley in East Yorkshire is a peaceful market town known primarily for its Medieval history and its imposing 13th century Minster, one of Europe's finest surviving gothic churches. Today Beverley hosts many food and music festivals and celebrated horse races on its famous track.

The pretty cobbled streets of Beverley are bustling with activity and are popular for their boutiques and acclaimed restaurants. The medieval food market sells crafts alongside cheeses, meats and other local produce. If you love music, the Beverley Folk festival is an entertaining yearly addition to the town's calendar.

CONTACT

34 Butcher Row
HU17 0AB
01482 391672

Cannon Hall Farm

PLACES TO VISIT | CAWTHORNE | S75 4AT

Cannon Hall Farm is a working farm with a family friendly focus. Adventure playgrounds, restaurants and its award-winning farm shop are all on site. Its popular, contemporary farm shop with a bakery, butchery and grocer, has been beautifully designed to display delicious home grown ingredients and local produce, using traditional methods of production.

Cannon Hall Farm Shop has won multiple awards. Artisan breads are baked daily alongside their famous pies, quiches and desserts. The farm shop deli is brimming with cheese, charcuterie and olives. Wines and local micro breweries' produce are also available.

CONTACT

Bark House Lane
S75 4AT
01226 790427

Cedarbarn Farm

PLACES TO VISIT | **PICKERING** | **YO18 7JX**

Their aim at Cedarbarn Farm is "to bring you top-quality, healthy, fresh food with impeccable provenance and as few food miles as possible". Inspired by their love of farming, they say they care deeply about their impact on the environment and try to operate in an eco-friendly way wherever possible.

The farm puts an emphasis on education and the welfare of their animals. With a miniature Victorian railway, you can hop aboard the 'Flying Yorkshireman' for a trip around the fruit fields and even stop off to pick your own soft fruit when it's in season. There is an award-winning cafe and farmshop on site.

CONTACT

Thornton Road
YO18 7JX
01751 475614

Goathland

PLACES TO VISIT | GOATHLAND | YO22 5LX

Goathland is a refreshing moorland village in the center of the North York National Park. The village has become increasingly popular as a tourist destination due to its role as Aidensfield in the TV series Heartbeat. Lots of old cars and business names are the same as in the series and a delight for Heartbeat enthusiasts.

More recently Goathland train station was used as the station for Hogsmeade in the first Harry Potter films. You can arrive in the village in the same manner as the students via steam train before taking in the sights.

CONTACT

The Green
YO22 5LX

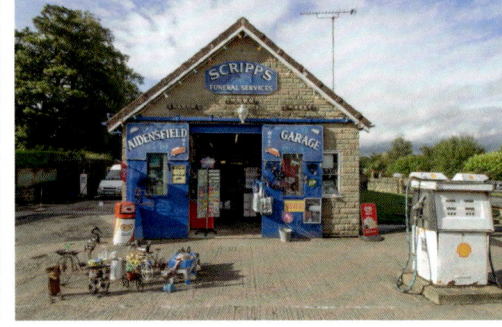

Harrogate

PLACES TO VISIT | HARROGATE | HG1 2WJ

The elegant, Victorian spa town of Harrogate was famous for its healing, mineral spring water. During the 17th and 18th centuries, Harrogate became a spa town destination. Today the town celebrates its history and offers abundant floral gardens, a respected theatre and quality, independent boutiques.

Harrogate is one of Yorkshire's most sophisticated towns. The Royal Pump Room, now a museum, built by Isaac Shutt in 1842, provided shelter for the town's affluent visitors that took the 'curing' waters. Visit Betty's Tearoom, renowned for its exceptional, traditional afternoon teas.

CONTACT

Royal Baths, Crescent Rd
HG1 2WJ
01423 537300

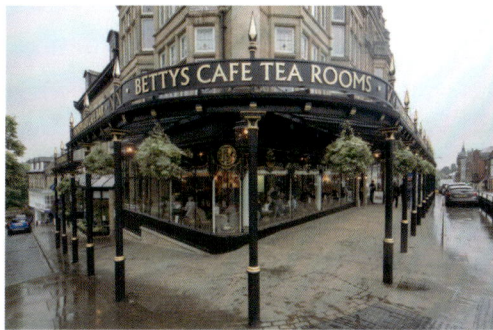

Staithes Fishing Village

YORKSHIRE

Humber Bridge

PLACES TO VISIT | HESSLE | HU13 0JG

The Humber Bridge is currently the longest single-span suspension bridge in the world to cycle or walk across. Grade 1 listed, this iconic structure links Lincolnshire and Yorkshire on the A15. Standing at 1.4-miles long, the bridge was opened in 1981 and created a faster route between the two banks of the Humber.

The Humber Bridge helped to realise the area's potential in terms of its commercial, industrial and tourist opportunities, which were previously limited. During the peak time of its build, there were one thousand people working on its construction, which took eight years to complete.

CONTACT

Ferriby Road
HU13 0JG
01482 647161

Pateley Bridge

PLACES TO VISIT | PATELEY BRIDGE | HG3 5AW

Situated in the heart of Nidderdale, an Area of Outstanding Natural Beauty, Pateley Bridge is the perfect point to start your exploration of the Yorkshire Dales. Renowned for its beautiful scenery, this market town offers tea rooms, restaurants and quaint boutiques which include England's Oldest Sweetshop.

Pateley Bridge is the start and finishing point of the circular Nidderdale way, a 53 mile route around the Nidd Valley, popular with walkers. The Nidderdale Museum, based in an original Victorian workhouse, depicts a traditional Yorkshire way of life, for those that like a little history.

CONTACT

18 High Street
HG3 5AW
01423 711147

Pickering

PLACES TO VISIT | PICKERING | YO18 7AJ

Located in the historic market town of Pickering is the themed Pickering Station. The station has a wonderful old feeling to it and has recently had a replacement roof installed, which was a design from the 1840's.

Steam trains operate throughout the year and are more frequent during the warmer months. As well as regular journeys between Whitby, Levisham, Grosmont and Goathland you can also book a dining car experience, where you can enjoy lunch, afternoon tea and dinner on board the Pullman Dining Train. This is a wonderful way to see the North York Moors in complete comfort.

CONTACT

Park Street
YO18 7AJ

RHS Garden Harlow Carr

PLACES TO VISIT | HARROGATE | HG3 1QB

RHS Garden Harlow Carr encompasses 68 acres of stunning growing landscapes, from running and still water to woodland and wildflower meadows. Famous for their rhododendrons and Himalayan blue poppies, the gardens are considered a showcase of horticultural excellence.

The innovative planning of the gardens at RHS Garden Harlow Carr is exceptional and includes concepts from a 'Scented Garden' with an emphasis on rose, jasmine and wisteria varieties to an inspiring 'Kitchen Garden' with fruit trees and abundant raised beds. From streamside walks to guided tours, the gardens provide visitors with enchanting beauty.

CONTACT
Crag Lane
HG3 1QB
01423 565418

Richmond

PLACES TO VISIT | RICHMOND | DL10 4DN

Described as the gateway to the Yorkshire Dales, Richmond, situated on the edge of the Yorkshire Dales National Park, is a town of scenic beauty which has long provided inspiration for painters and poets. Founded by the Normans in 1071 the town developed around the castle built on the 'riche-mont' or 'strong-hill' which gave the town its name.

Richmond's cobbled market place is surrounded by Georgian properties, created when the town flourished during this era. Richmond's castle was one of the greatest Norman fortresses in Britain and its impressive remains are a popular place to visit.

CONTACT

Richmond Library, Queens Rd
DL10 4DN
01609 532980

Ripon

PLACES TO VISIT | RIPON | HG4 1BP

The city of Ripon, founded 1300 years ago, is located in North Yorkshire on the River Ure. This pretty market town is celebrated as a Cathedral City, where monasteries have stood since the 7th Century. With a popular market and a famous horse-racing track, Ripon also offers an abundance of boutiques, restaurants and cafes.

Ripon is situated at the foot of the Yorkshire Dales and is another good base to explore the surrounding countryside. Ripon Cathedral is architecturally stunning, with a fascinating history. Inside, its majestic stained glass window with its vivid colours, is impressive.

CONTACT
Market Pl S
HG4 1BP
01765 604625

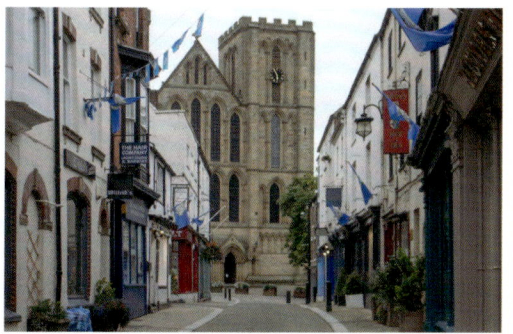
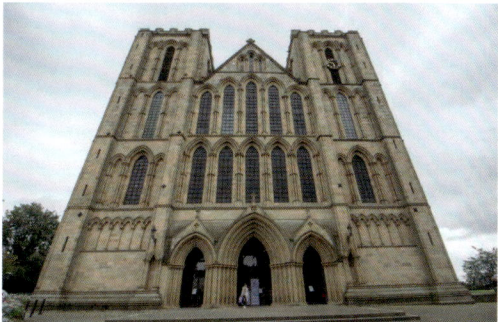

Robin Hood's Bay

PLACES TO VISIT | ROBIN HOOD'S BAY | YO22 4SJ

Robin Hood's Bay is a rustic coastal area in Yorkshire, loved for its rugged and inspiring beauty. Old fisherman cottages and ancient inns are sprinkled around this scenic bay, which attracts walkers, horse riders and those that enjoy the water. There are also good cafes and restaurants specialising in seafood and cream teas in this area.

Historically Robin Hood's Bay was known as Baytown and was at the heart of smuggling operations for alcohol, tobacco and French lace in the 18th century. Today, fossil hunting is a favourite family activity on the beach, as the area is known for its Jurassic period rocks.

CONTACT
New Road
YO22 4SJ

Rosedale Abbey

PLACES TO VISIT | PICKERING | YO18 8SA

Once a thriving home to 5000 ironstone miners, Rosedale Abbey was a bustling industrial town after the ironstone discovery around 1850. The ruins are not from those of an Abbey as the town's name suggests but more likely the remains of a Cistercian Priory, inhabited by nuns from 1158.

During the mining era, the priory stone was taken and used to build a new church on the site of the original priory. Today, the old Priory is still evident outside of The Church of St Mary and St Laurence. The pictureque landscape here makes Rosedale Abbey a popular choice with walkers.

CONTACT

Rosedale Abbey
YO18 8SA

Rosedale Abbey, North Yorkshire

BY RICHARD BOWDEN

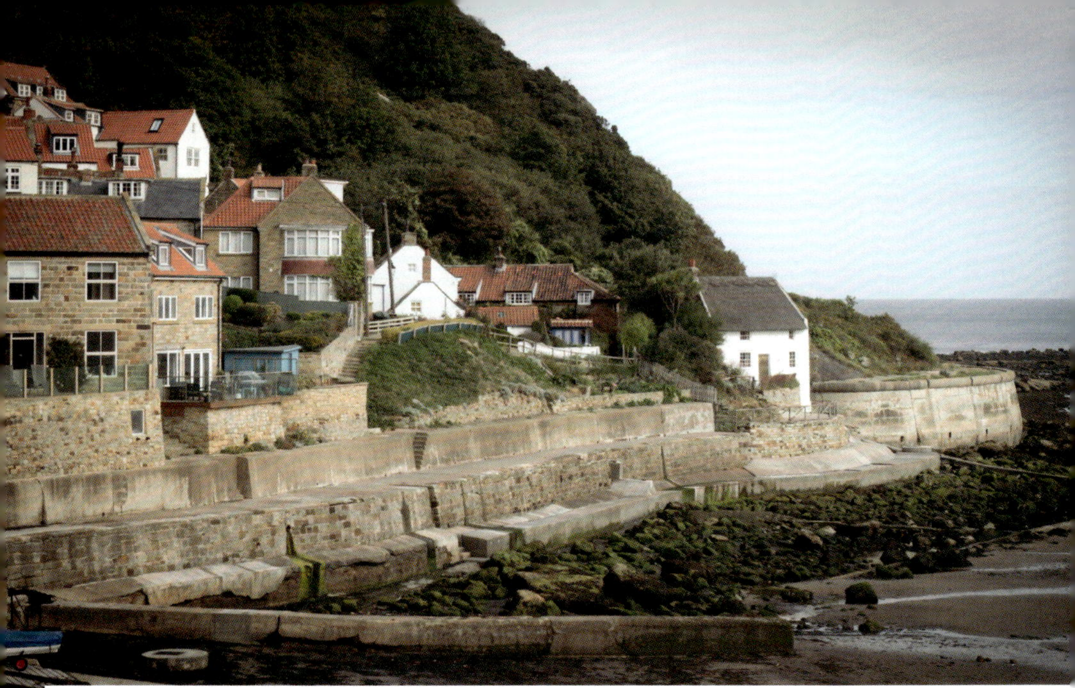

Runswick Bay

PLACES TO VISIT | RUNSWICK BAY | TS13 5HT

Runswick Bay is a popular family destination on a dramatic section of coast. Rock pooling, fossil hunting and blustery coastal walks are popular activities in this area. The peaceful sandy bay offers great surfing and sailing opportunities and is set against the charming village backdrop of red roofed cottages.

The old RNLI lifeboat station was operational until the late 1970s and today offers incredible panoramic views over the water. For walking and outdoor enthusiasts, there are a multitude of scenic coastal paths and trails in the Runswick Bay area.

CONTACT

Cleveland Way
TS13 5HT

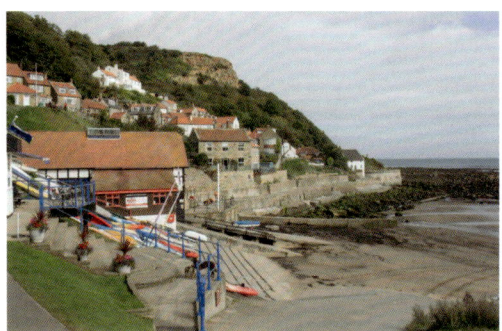

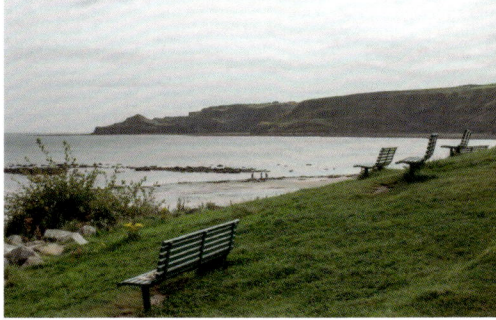

Saltburn-by-the-Sea

PLACES TO VISIT | SALTBURN-BY-THE-SEA | TS12 1NY

Saltburn by the Sea is a laid back, Victorian seaside town renowned for its slow pace and surfing. Its Victorian pier has survived almost 150 years of extreme weather, as England's most northerly pier and the town itself is proud of its smuggling past and celebrated Victorian constructions, from its railway to its cliff lift.

The town became popular in the 1870s with industrialists wanting to escape to the tranquil coastal resort of Saltburn by the Sea, with its fresh air and relaxed environment. The Cliff Lift is still operational today, taking visitors from the steep cliff to the beach.

CONTACT

Saltburn Road
TS12 1NY

Scarborough

PLACES TO VISIT | SCARBOROUGH | YO11 1JW

Scarborough has been a go-to holiday destination in the UK for almost 400 years. Two bays with glorious golden sand offer a great day out for all the family. The South Bay is filled with sparkly amusement arcades and spade shops, whereas the North Bay is much quieter with rows of colourful beach huts and a waterpark.

Scarborough's harbour and old town are particularly attractive with cobbled streets and a miss-match of buildings that gradually make their way uphill. We recommend a trek to Olivers on the Mount for excellent views over the castle and bay, great for a hot drink after a walk.

CONTACT
Stephen Joseph Theatre
YO11 1JW
01723 383636

Skipton

PLACES TO VISIT | SKIPTON | BD23 1AH

The scenic, market town of Skipton is situated in the foothills of the Dales and has won numerous awards for its popular high street and the happiness of its inhabitants. Its spellbinding, medieval castle is over 900 years old and beautifully preserved and maintained.

Surrounded by serene landscape, Skipton has a plethora of coffee shops, restaurants and cafes, nestled amongst the cobbled streets and stone terraces. Boat trips can be taken on the pretty canal which travels through the town, passing many of its pubs and eateries.

CONTACT

High Street
BD23 1AH
01756 792809

The Carding Shed

PLACES TO VISIT | HEPWORTH | HD9 1AF

The Carding Shed is a nostalgic trip down memory lane. This retro themed experience, situated in a beautiful former mill showcases a vintage car collection and cafe which has become hugely popular with car enthusiasts. Bicycles hang amongst vintage signage, bunting and other eccentric decorative details.

The Carding Shed's Oil Can Cafe is open for breakfast, lunch and an indulgent afternoon tea. Drink from vintage china tea cups and enjoy their home-baked cakes and warm scones. The cafe prides itself on using locally sourced ingredients. Retro themed gifts and clothing are also sold at The Carding Shed.

CONTACT
Butt Lane
HD9 1AF
01484 680300

Thomason Foss Waterfall

PLACES TO VISIT | GOATHLAND | YO22 5LE

A short walk from The Birch Hall Inn is the beautiful Thomason Foss Waterfall. If you turn left out of the pub and left again up the path you'll be sure to reach it. It can be wet underfoot and a bit of a scramble in places however you are rewarded with a collection of falls and wonderful woodlands.

If wild swimming is your thing then head on in, there is a plunge pool 20 meters deep directly beneath the main falls where you'll often see the locals jumping from the top. Warm up with tasty grub from the pub after a rewarding drink.

CONTACT

Beck Hole Road
YO22 5LE

Thornton le Dale

PLACES TO VISIT | THORNTON LE DALE | YO18 7LG

Thornton Le Dale has won countless awards for being Britain's most attractive town, with its thatched cottages, gentle stream running alongside the Main Street and pretty gardens. The village is certainly picturesque and highly photographed; you might have seen the thatched cottage by the 'babbling beck' on a number of chocolate boxes and sweet selections.

We recommend having a gentle stroll through the village, followed by a bite from Balderson's bakery. A visit to Thornton Dale wouldn't be complete without stocking up on goodies from The Chocolate Factory, where mouth-watering treats are plentiful.

CONTACT
Pickering Road
YO18 7LG

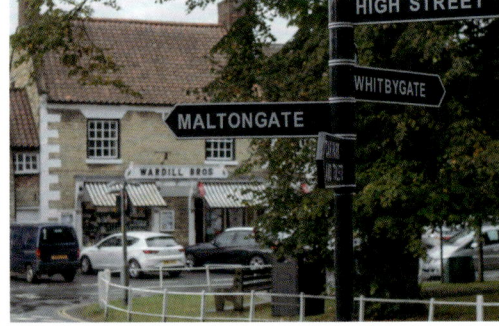

Whitby

PLACES TO VISIT | WHITBY | YO21 1DN

Situated at the mouth of the river Esk on Yorkshire's East coast, Whitby is a traditional seaside resort and port with an interesting history and scenic views. With an active local fishing industry making use of the port, restaurants specialising in seafood and Fish and Chips are nationally renowned.

Captain Cook moved to Whitby to become a trainee with a local shipping firm and the house where he lodged is now a museum dedicated to him, as one of the world's greatest explorers. The remains of the abbey high on the cliff and the cottages that wind their way down to the sea only enhance Whitby's scenic qualities.

CONTACT
Langborne Rd
YO21 1DN
01723 383636

Whitby Harbourside

YORKSHIRE

York

PLACES TO VISIT | YORK | YO1 7DT

York is a picturesque, riverside city brimming with fascinating history and cosmopolitan charm. Its famous walls, impressive architecture and cobbled streets, create an awe inspiring backdrop to this popular city. The striking stained glass windows in the Gothic Cathedral captivate visitors with their resplendent vibrancy.

York's history extends back over two thousand years as a Roman settlement and it has managed to preserve so many of its historic features over the centuries. Juxtaposed against its famous landmarks are an array of chic boutiques, coffee shops, fine dining eateries and respected galleries.

CONTACT
1 Museum Street
YO1 7DT
01904 550099

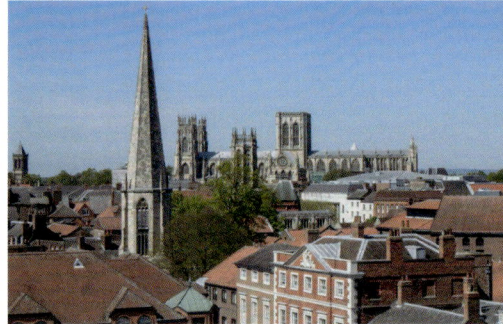

Yorkshire Dales

PLACES TO VISIT | YORKSHIRE | BD23 5LB

With spectacular waterfalls, cascading hills, broadleaved woodland and meadowland flora, The Yorkshire Dales are one of England's most revered natural environments. Home to little stone villages and traditional farmland, the Dales (valleys) are ever-changing throughout the seasons.

The Yorkshire Dales are popular with outdoor enthusiasts. The scenic Settle to Carlisle railway carves through the National Park with its beautifully constructed viaducts, including the iconic Ribblehead. The Three Peaks of Pen-y-ghent, Ingleborough and Whernside are among the best known hills in the Yorkshire Dales National Park.

CONTACT

Hebden Rd, Grassington
BD23 5LB
01756 751690

BEST OF ENGLAND

PUBS

YORKSHIRE

Birch Hall Inn

PUB | **GOATHLAND** | **YO22 5LE**

The tiny, historic pub of Birch Hall is situated in the village of Beck Hole, named from the Viking description of 'a deep valley through which runs a stream'. The pub can be traced back to the 1600s and its walls are lined with traditional wallpaper. The worn wooden mismatched tables and chairs have not much changed over the years of ownership.

Birch Hall Inn is a pub visited by walkers, locals and those that appreciate its untouched charm. Situated next to the bridge over the ford, the pub serves a few bar snacks such as 'pork pie and pickle' from the local butcher and a handful of locally produced beers.

CONTACT

Beck Hole Road
YO22 5LE
01947 896245

Black Sheep Brewery

PUB | MASHAM | HG4 4EN

Paul Theakston founded The Black Sheep Brewery in 1992 after following his passion and deep rooted family connection to beer brewing. Since then it has built an impressive reputation for crafting fine, experimental beers and ales. Set in Masham, North Yorkshire, Black Sheep produces cask, keg and bottled beers.

With expertise spanning six generations, the brewery offers a fascinating tour. After learning about its interesting history and the ins and outs of how the brewery runs, why not enjoy an indulgent burger and chips in their busy Black Sheep Bistro with one of the Black Sheep Brewery beers.

CONTACT

Wellgarth
HG4 4EN
01765 689227

Craven Arms

PUB | APPLETREEWICK | BD23 6DA

The Craven Arms in Appletreewick is a picture-postcard, old English pub, with a great reputation for its food and real ale. The ale is all traditionally cask-conditioned and the artisan dishes are lovingly prepared from local ingredients on the premises.

The Craven Arms began its life as a 16th century farm house and many of its original features remain. Open fires create a cozy atmosphere and on warmer days, you can enjoy views of the spectacular scenery from the garden. The pub has its own herb garden and the thatched Cruck Barn hosts many events and functions.

CONTACT

Craven Arms
BD23 6DA
01756 720270

Mill Hey Brew House

PUB | **HAWORTH** | **BD22 8NQ**

Specialising in great beer, delicious fresh cocktails and Barista coffee, Mill Hey Brew House has an almost industrial style interior with pendant lighting, exposed metal beams and stone flooring. Leather chesterfield armchairs and sofas soften the ambience, as does the wooden bar and woodburning stove.

Its contemporary ambience and live music events make the Mill Hey Brew House a popular choice with a younger crowd. Metal bar stools, high ceilings and large, light-filled windows add to the modern appeal of this pub.

CONTACT

2 Mill Hey
BD22 8NQ
01535 646823

Summer Wine Brewery Tap

PUB | **HONLEY** | HD9 6PL

Summer Wine Brewery Tap is on a mission to revolutionise Yorkshire beer by redefining its perception. They plan to put Yorkshire beer on the map in a different way, by brewing avante garde beers that make people think twice about what they have accepted as the standard when it comes to beer.

Attached to the brewery is a contemporary bar space where their beers can be sampled. With good tunes, a warehouse aesthetic, vibrant vintage signage and wooden benches, the team behind Summer Wine Brewery Tap are determined to give beer a less traditional face and they are succeeding.

CONTACT

Unit 15 Crossley Mills, New Mill Road

HD9 6PL

01484 665466

Sausage & Mash

England has a proud history of butchery and you'll find many independent merchants present on high streets nationwide to this day. A plate of sausages and buttery mashed potatoes is the perfect way to taste the tradition.

As butchers increasingly value heritage breeds, the dish receives a flavour twist, with venison or rare breed meat flavouring the sausage.

The Angel Inn

PUB | SKIPTON | BD23 6LT

The Angel was bought in 1983 by "the Godfather of the Gastropub" Denis Watkins who took chips off the menu in 1985 and instead served every dish with mangetout and fresh new potatoes. Since that time it has gone from strength to strength and is well recognised in the Dales as one of the top eateries.

With nine en-suite rooms and a choice of either bar food or the more formal restaurant, serving French Yorkshire cuisine, you're spoilt for choice at The Angel Inn. Parts of the Inn are over 500 years old, so you can expect old-age charm and character.

CONTACT

Hetton
BD23 6LT
01756 730263

The Black Bull

PUB | MIDDLEHAM | DL8 4NX

The Black Bull is situated in the town of Middleham in North Yorkshire and prides itself on its good quality food and welcoming atmosphere. The pub is in an ideal base for walking and cycling in an area renowned for its history and scenery. Middleham castle is a popular attraction for visitors here.

The interior of The Black Bull is unfussy with light and contemporary tones, stone floors, an open fire and wooden tables. The picturesque Wensleydale countryside surrounds the pub and offers walkers of varying experience beautiful hikes amongst the ever changing landscape.

CONTACT

Market Place
DL8 4NX
01969 624792

Steamed Mussels

Often served simply to fill a deep bowl with their glistening inky shells, mussels make a hearty meal and are excellent when accompanied by a white wine or garlic sauce.

They are also great additions to a seafood chowder, although not all mussels are harvested from the sea – there are freshwater varieties, too. Blue mussels are England's most common variety.

The Blue Lion

PUB | LEYBURN | DL8 4SN

Sturdy oak tables, roaring log fires and old English charm create the setting for the award-winning Blue Lion in Leyburn. Their freshly prepared, seasonal menu is regionally renowned and their hand-pulled ales range from local classics to interesting guest varieties.

Surrounded by the beautiful Yorkshire Dales National Park, the historic 18th century Blue Lion Inn offers both a traditional pub setting alongside a more formal, candlelit dining room with its red and green colour palette, stripped wooden floors and elegant rugs. Quality, tradition and friendliness are at the heart of the family-run Blue Lion.

CONTACT

Main Road
DL8 4SN
01969 624273

The Bull at Broughton

PUB | SKIPTON | BD23 3AE

Known for its great food, the Bull at Broughton is popular for its contemporary take on traditional and local dishes. Only using the finest, regional and artisanal ingredients, the Bull has long been the place to come for a relaxing, quality dining experience. The character, atmosphere and beautiful surrounding countryside only enhance the experience.

With regional Cask Ales and an award-winning wine list, The Bull at Broughton has a cozy, contemporary interior with original features including a flagstone floor, open fire and dark wood beams. The pub terrace garden is a welcome addition on warmer days.

CONTACT

Broughton
BD23 3AE
01756 792065

The Butchers Arms

PUB | **HEPWORTH** | HD9 1TE

The Butchers Arms is a traditional old stone pub in the heart of the village of Hepworth. Its menu is influenced by French cuisine but the ingredients are very much sourced locally from Yorkshire. While friendliness and service are the pub's ethos, the food has gained a reputation for its excellence.

Chef Mark Hogan has spent much of his life travelling the world. Before moving to Yorkshire he spent five years immersed in France and has brought his expertise and passion for French cuisine to The Butchers Arms.

CONTACT

38 Town Gate
HD9 1TE
01484 687147

The Devonshire Grassington

PUB | **GRASSINGTON** | **BD23 5AD**

The Devonshire is a traditional pub with vibrant, contemporary furnishings. Situated on pretty Grassington Square, its stone facade and central positioning makes the pub popular with locals and visitors alike. Woodburners and soft furnishings create a comfortable environment and the menu offers traditional pub dishes.

Lilac colour tones and silver grey highlights paint the interior, whilst pops of green and red appear on comfy leather chesterfield chairs. The Devonshire offers guest rooms in a similar contemporary style to the pub, with light furnishings and comfort at the heart of their design.

CONTACT

27 Main Street
BD23 5AD
01756 752 525

Raw Oysters

Head to the South East to sample some of England's finest oysters in season. Heralded as the ultimate seafood treat, the process of eating one is far from elegant as you lift the oyster – shell and all – and gulp the contents down.

Despite being so distinctive, raw oysters pair well with a surprising range of flavours, from tangy lemon to ginger and peppers.

The Dunkirk

PUB | **DENBY DALE** | **HD8 8TX**

The Dunkirk in Denby Dale is a beautifully renovated pub with a roof terrace which maximises the views of the scenic local area. With natural light spilling through the windows and a colour palette of light, silvery greys and pale woods, the interior is more fine dining than country pub.

The menu at The Dunkirk focuses on the quality of its locally sourced, seasonal ingredients. The drinks menu celebrates the resurgence in popularity of real ale and local gins with a plethora of local microbreweries featured. Wine is sourced carefully with Denby Dale Wines to enrich your dining experience.

CONTACT
231 Barnsley Road
HD8 8TX
01484 862912

The Fountaine Inn

PUB | LINTON | BD23 5HJ

The Fountaine Inn is a pub with personality. Situated in the stunning Yorkshire countryside, this inn is about community and great hospitality. Its stylish interior fuses modern with traditional, with a fun mix of textures, colours and patterns to create a vibrant atmosphere.

From imaginative recipes to simple pub classics, the menu at The Fountaine Inn sources local ingredients from suppliers in the region. The open fires create a cozy environment and guest rooms with a similar contemporary style, within the pub's traditional surroundings are also available.

CONTACT

Linton in Craven
BD23 5HJ
01756 752210

The Kings Head

PUB | **KETTLEWELL** | BD23 5RD

The Kings Head at Kettlewell is an exceptional and award-winning pub with national recognition for its food and accommodation. Surrounded by some of Yorkshire's most scenic countryside, The Kings Head's menu specialises in a modern approach to traditional British pub classics.

People come from far and wide to taste the delicious and traditional yet refined dishes at The Kings Head. The pub's interior is light and contemporary with original character features including the fireplaces and stone flooring, which compliment the soft neutral and ambient colour scheme. There are five en-suite guest rooms.

CONTACT

The Green
BD23 5RD
01756 761600

The Lister Arms

PUB | MALHAM | BD23 4DB

The Lister Arms in Malham is a traditional coaching inn with captivating period features and an exterior embellished in vibrant green foliage. The inn's interior has been modernised whilst retaining its rich history and features, from its beams and wooden floors to its original fireplaces.

Local, seasonal ingredients from trusted suppliers are the focus of the traditional menu at The Lister Arms in Malham. Particularly popular with walkers, due to its idyllic position within the Yorkshire Dales, the inviting ambience and roaring log fires make this a great spot to stop for food or a drink.

CONTACT

Malham
BD23 4DB
01729 830330

199 steps from St Mary's Church

WHITBY HARBOUR, YORKSHIRE

The Old Hall Inn

PUB | **GRASSINGTON** | **BD23 5HB**

The Old Hall Inn in Threshfield in the heart of the Yorkshire Dales is a friendly and traditional pub. They pride themselves on making all of their food in-house using local, seasonal ingredients. Everything is made by their chefs, from their breads to their ice cream.

Accommodation at The Old Hall Inn consists of four en-suite rooms and additionally a 14th century cottage, reportedly the oldest habitable building in the Yorkshire Dales, with it's history traced back to the 14th century. The pub is in walking distance of the picturesque village of Grassington, and the famous Linton Falls.

CONTACT

Main Street
BD23 5HB
01756 752441

The Queens Arms

PUB | SKIPTON | BD23 5QJ

The beautiful 17th century Queens Arms in Litton in the Yorkshire Dales puts an emphasis on its food, drinks and staff being 'locally sourced'. A recent refurbishment has retained the pub's original features including its slate floors, stone walls and open fires whilst introducing a contemporary, soft colour scheme combined with country chic fabrics and furnishings.

The Queens Arms is a great base for walkers, with the "3 peaks" all within easy reach. The pub even has a very handy drying room for boots and coats. Six guest rooms are also available, providing a simple, modern style.

CONTACT

Litton
BD23 5QJ
01756 770096

The Pork Pie

The classic pork pie originates from
the characterful Leicestershire town of
Melton Mowbray – amble along the
shopping streets to enjoy the smell of
pork pies cooking wafting from
bakeries.

The dish itself is deliciously simple,
made from hot water crust pastry, jelly
and pork. Luxury takes on this cold pie
often include hard-boiled egg centres
or game meat.

The Richard III

PUB | **MIDDLEHAM** | **DL8 4NP**

The Richard III Hotel is named after Middleham's most famous resident, who spent time in the castle behind the pub. Mentioned in the Domesday Book, Middleham is steeped in history, and this 17th century pub has been a central part of life here for over 300 years. Its excellent position is ideal for visiting the castle.

Paintings with an equestrian and racing theme are combined with eccentric furnishings and fairy lights which all highlight the walls of The Richard III. The menu presents traditional pub fare with their meat sourced from local butchers.

CONTACT

Market Place
DL8 4NP
01969 623240

The Sandpiper Inn

PUB | **LEYBURN** | DL8 5AT

The Sandpiper Inn is an award-winning gastro pub situated in the glorious market town of Leyburn. This fine, historic, 17th century inn prides itself on its locally sourced, fine food. The dining room has stripped wooden flooring and a deep, serene green interior contrasting against the original beams.

The Stubbing Wharf

PUB | **HEBDEN BRIDGE** | HX7 6LU

Popular with walkers and locals, The Stubbing Wharf was refurbished after a devastating flood in the area and has come back stronger. With many of the original pub features preserved, the new interior style adds a little country chic to this beautifully positioned pub. Traditional pub dishes feature on the menu.

The Tempest Arms

PUB | **SKIPTON** | BD23 3AY

Once you've managed to find the little hamlet of Elslack, head for the Tempest Arms, the epitome of the country inn. Dating back to the 17th century, the Tempest is a landmark in the area and known for its convivial atmosphere, log fires and real ales. Their menu focuses on classic roasts and slow cooked meats.

The White Hart Inn

PUB | **HAWES** | DL8 3QL

The White Hart Country Inn is a 16th Century Coaching Inn, situated on a cobbled street in the market town of Hawes. It has been sympathetically renovated to retain the atmosphere and charm of its traditional heritage but with a contemporary twist. Open fires and woodburners are cozy for when walkers return from their hikes.

The White Lion

PUB | HEBDEN BRIDGE | HX7 8EX

The White Lion is a beautifully restored inn situated in a riverside position in Hebden Bridge. Chic country fabrics, polished wooden floors and roaring log fires make this a favourite spot to enjoy delicious, locally sourced cuisine. Exposed stone, wood cladding and candlelight create a cozy and intimate atmosphere.

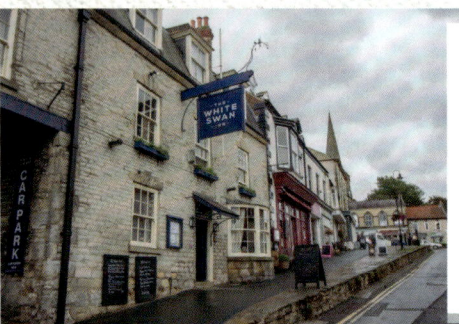

The White Swan Inn

PUB | PICKERING | YO18 7AA

Situated in the historic market town of Pickering, The White Swan is a traditional 16th century coaching inn offering the perfect rural retreat with its focus on relaxed luxury. Soft neutral colours, leather and wood furnishings and cozy log fires all create an indulgent ambience.

The Yorkshire Terrier

PUB | YORK | YO1 8AS

Situated on historic Stonegate in the centre of York, The Yorkshire Terrier is positioned behind their York Brewery gift shop. The pub is compact and traditional in style with an excellent selection of ales. This city centre pub is an easy stop off after enjoying the historic sites of the city.

Waggon & Horses

PUB | OXENHOPE | BD22 9QE

The Waggon & Horses pub is situated in an elevated position boasting some of Yorkshire's finest views. Their ethos is to create 'a proper country dining experience in a relaxed and atmospheric environment.' The pub is steeped in history from when it was founded around the 1850s and many of its original features remain.

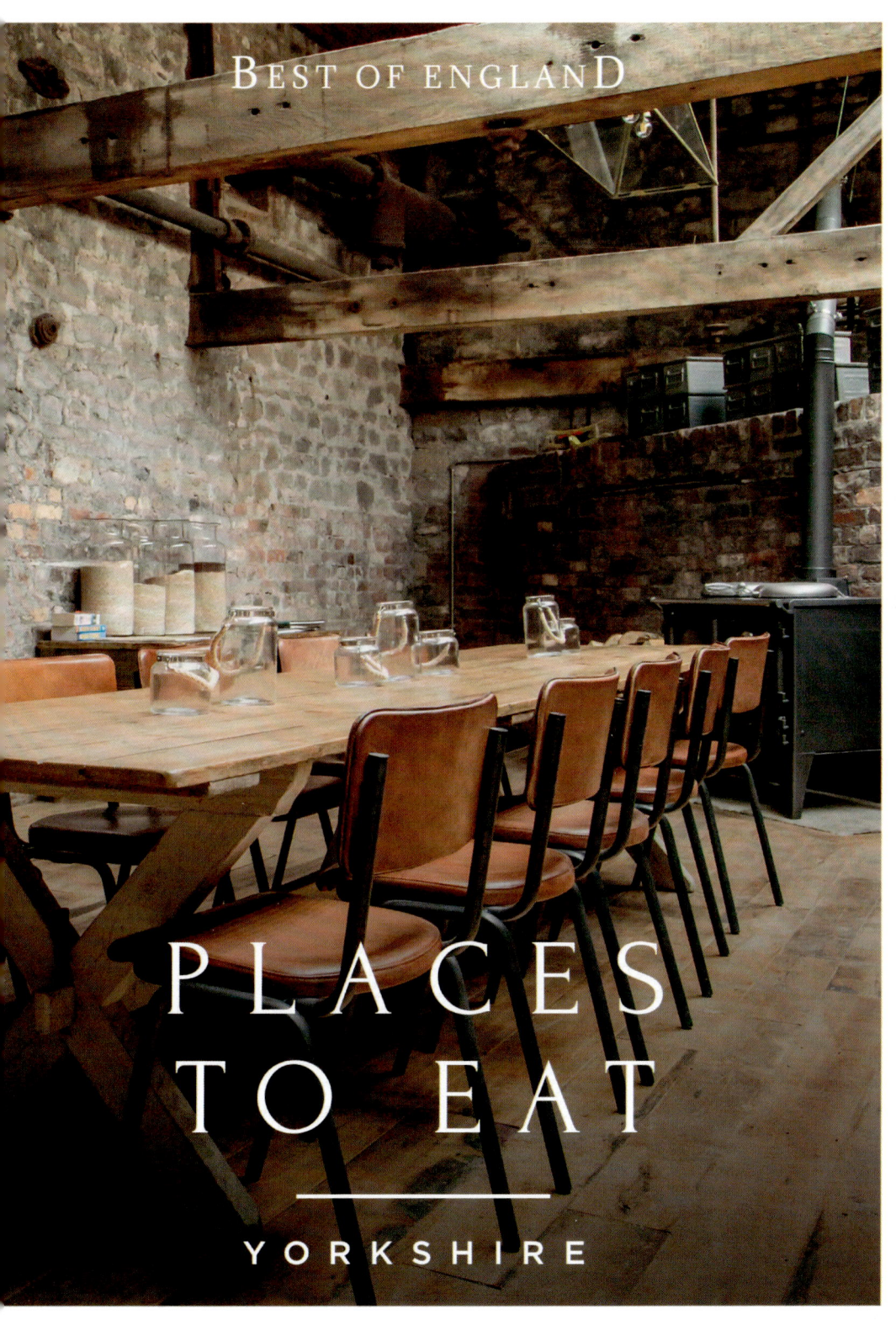

PLACES TO EAT

YORKSHIRE

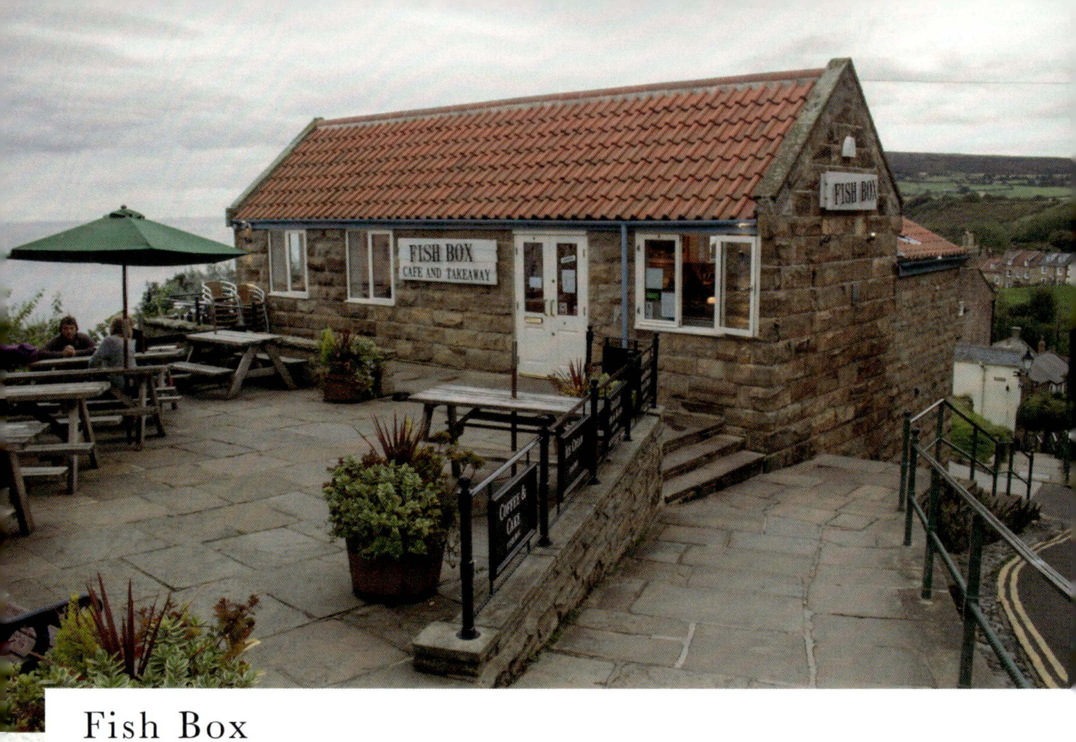

Fish Box

PLACES TO EAT | ROBIN HOOD'S BAY | YO22 4SE

Fish Box is beautifully located restaurant in the heart of Robin Hood's Bay at the top of Bay Bank. Situated at the top of the cliff, it has impressive panoramic views across the Bay. This light and contemporary cafe serves sustainably sourced, high quality fish and chips.

With white washed wood cladded walls, brown leather banquettes, stripped wooden floors and brass pendant lighting, Fish Box acknowledges the region's fishing heritage with its black and white photography hanging on the walls. Cleverly amalgamating traditional values with a modern aesthetic, Fish Box is an extremely popular cafe.

CONTACT

Bay Bank
YO22 4SE
01947 880595

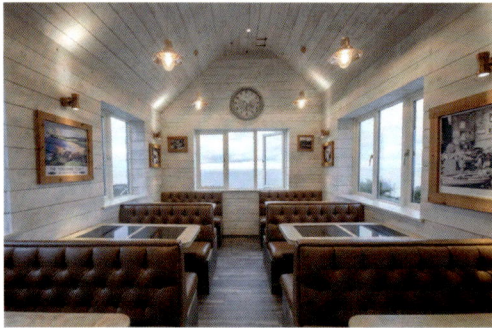

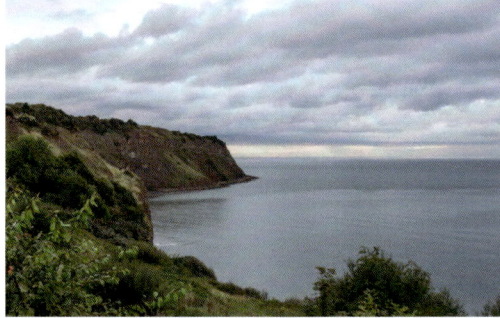

Hollins Mill

PLACES TO EAT | SOWERBY BRIDGE | HX6 2QG

Set in an impressive building which has been converted from a characterful Mill, Hollins Mill showcases its industrial heritage, with its enormous arched windows, exposed brickwork walls, timber and metal beams and large feature brick fireplace.

The pub has only recently become Hollins Mill after years of being The Works, so its reputation for its cuisine and drinks is embryonic. The building and its heritage is however interesting and offers a large, spacious environment with a laid back ambience to enjoy a drink.

CONTACT
12 Hollins Mill Lane
HX6 2QG
01422 647410

Goathland

BY CHRISTOPHER HOOD

Humble Pie 'N' Mash Shop

PLACES TO EAT | WHITBY | YO22 4AS

Humble Pie is a family run business, baking fresh home-made pies each day (with natural ingredients), all under the roof of their lovingly restored 16th century timber-framed shop. This traditional shop and cafe has a quirky, old-world interior with union jack bunting and a scattering of vintage inspired accessories.

With both meat and vegetarian options available on the menu at Humble Pie 'n' Mash, their pies can can be enjoyed on their own, or for a classic combination try with their mash, peas, and topped off with gravy. The pies are made from locally sourced produce.

CONTACT

163 Church Street
YO22 4AS
01947 606444

Rustique

PLACES TO EAT | RICHMOND | DL10 4QB

Rustique opened its doors in 2009, offering traditional French cuisine amongst its quirky Parisian-style surroundings. French food is served in this vibrant bistro restaurant and transports diners to the streets of Paris with its themed interior.

The à la carte, set menu and lunch menu offer a varied selection of meat and fish dishes cooked traditionally, using local ingredients. A carefully selected wine list offers a wide range of French and New World wines to complement the cuisine.

CONTACT

5-7 Chantry Wynd, Finkle Street
DL10 4QB
01748 821565

Six Poor Folk

PLACES TO EAT | KNARESBOROUGH | HG5 8AR

By day Six Poor Folk is a cosy coffee house and by night it transforms into a candlelit bistro, with an emphasis on using local suppliers to provide the highest level of quality, seasonal and fresh ingredients. The coffeehouse and bistro is a microwave free-zone which means their focus is on cooking to create impressive, flavoursome dishes rather than speed of customer turn-over, so you may need to wait.

Six Poor Folk is fully licensed and serves delicious coffee created uniquely for them by York Coffee Emporium. Their house blend is 'smooth and sweet with hints of ripe fruits and a dark cocoa after taste.'

CONTACT
25 Castlegate
HG5 8AR
01423 869918

The Belted Bull

PLACES TO EAT | CHOP GATE | TS9 7JH

Lord Stones Country Park is a destination location that will immerse you in the beauty of North York Moors National Park. With glamping, a cafe, farm shop and restaurant, the breathtaking views and walking opportunities make this a nature-lover's paradise. The peaceful and secluded glamping pods make camping comfortable for those who enjoy embracing nature with a little comfort!

The Belted Bull restaurant at Lord Stones focuses on the highest quality, seasonal produce. The cozy woodburning stove and friendly staff create a relaxing and casual atmosphere. Their beef is renowned for its excellence.

CONTACT

Carlton Bank
TS9 7JH
01642 778482

Norland

BY CHRISTOPHER SMITH

The Box Tree

PLACES TO EAT | ILKLEY | LS29 9DR

The Box Tree is an iconic restaurant in Ilkley that has been serving award-worthy food for over 50 years. Dishes have classical French roots and are light and delicate. Since 2005 the restaurant has been awarded a Michelin star for excellence.

The Box Tree is an exquisite eating experience and offers an a la carte menu, plat du jour menus for both lunch and dinner, Sunday lunch menu and the special menu Gourmand. A visit to The Box Tree is ideal for a surprise or special occasion as although it is not cheap, it is memorable and food at its best.

CONTACT

35 Church Street
LS29 9DR
01943 608484

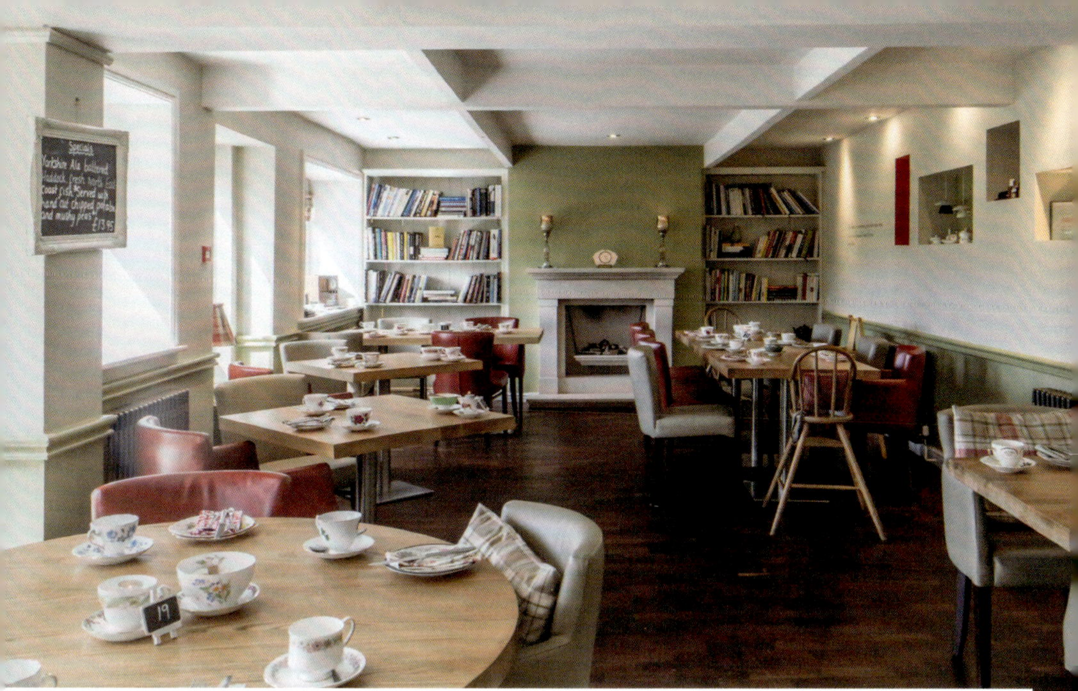

The Spiced Pear

PLACES TO EAT | HEPWORTH | HD9 7TP

The Spiced Pear is a Vintage Tea Room, Dining Room and Cocktail Bar complete with a grand piano and cozy open log fire. Renowned for its mouth-watering afternoon-teas served with indulgent warm scones that ooze Yorkshire clotted cream, the contemporary aesthetic creates an experience worlds away from the old-fashioned approach of most tea-rooms.

With far-reaching views from the terrace, The Spiced Pear has quality and presentation at the heart of their tearoom. Vintage china cups and saucers, flower embellished cake stands and many pretty details make this a popular spot for breakfast through to afternoon-tea.

CONTACT

Sheffield Road, New Mill
HD9 7TP
01484 683775

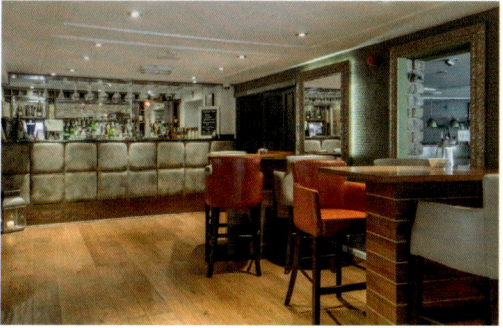

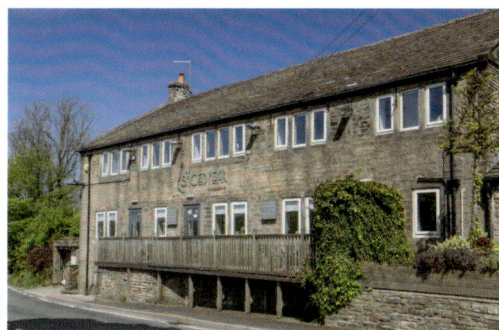

The Seaview

PLACES TO EAT | SALTBURN-BY-THE-SEA | TS12 1HQ

Overlooking the golden sands and dramatic cliffs of Saltburn-on-Sea, Seaview restaurant aims to serve the best fish and chips dining experience with views to match. Sourcing only the finest quality fish from sustainable and well mananged fishing grounds and respected fish merchants, quality is their focus.

With its nautically themed, contemporary interior, this light and airy restaurant also offers a balcony with stunning, panoramic views of the sea. Vibrant blue leather banquettes and sea-themed artwork set the scene while a suspended wooden kayak hangs from the ceiling.

CONTACT

Lower Promenade
TS12 1HQ
01287 626585

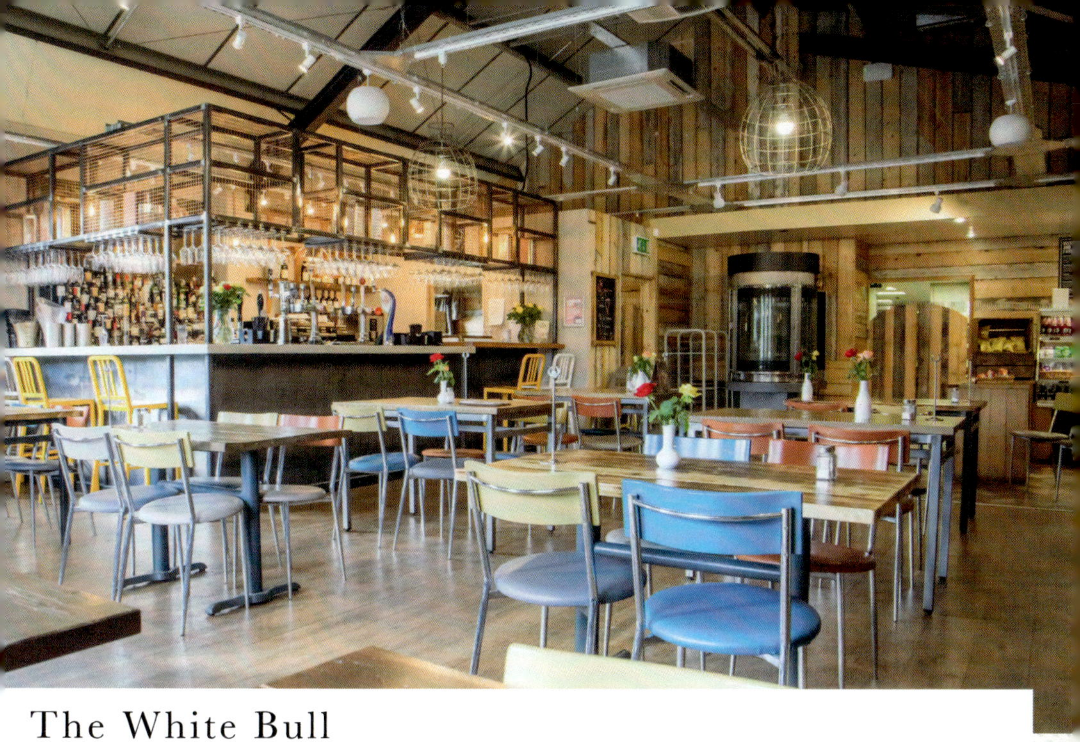

The White Bull

PLACES TO EAT | CAWTHORNE | S75 4AT

Situated at Cannon Hall Farm, The White Bull is named after Grandpa Nicholson's prize winning bull Sam, who enjoyed a pint in the beer tent after winning a prize at local shows. Casual food from sandwiches and baked potatoes to seafood baskets are served in this almost industrial style restaurant.

Wood features heavily with the interior styling and bright pops of vibrant blue and yellow highlight the furnishings. This family style restaurant is naturally popular with those visiting the farm, so is often lively. Table and booth seating are available.

CONTACT

Bark House Lane
S75 4AT
01226 790427

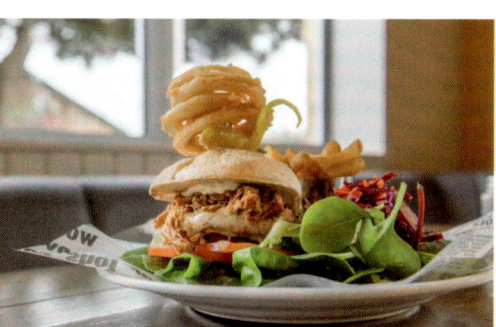

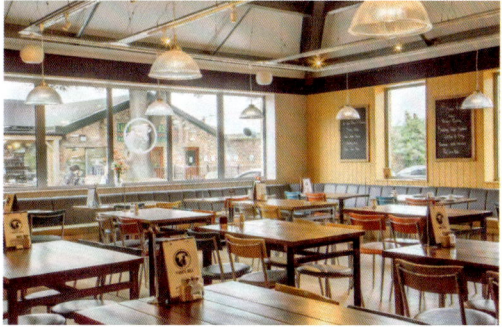

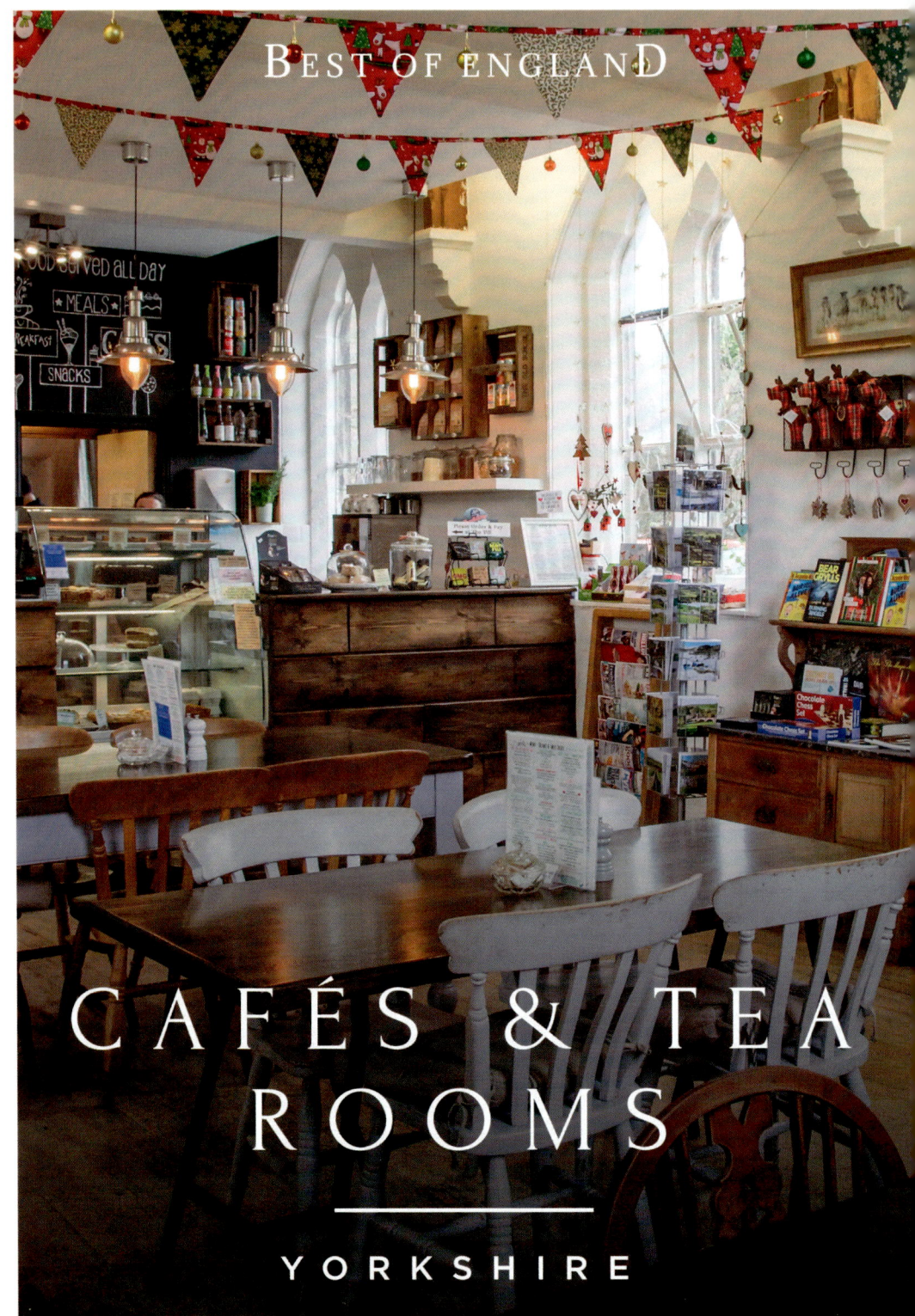

CAFÉS & TEA ROOMS

YORKSHIRE

The Dalesman Tearoom

CAFÉS & TEA ROOMS | GARGRAVE | BD23 3LX

The Dalesman Tearoom is a quirky and eclectic café and sweet emporium serving homemade food, cakes and traditional sweets. A fantastic array of vintage sweet tins decorate the walls and shelves whilst traditional sweet jars overflowing with kaleidoscopic candy are in abundance.

Popular with cyclists passing through, walkers and locals, the Dalesman Tearoom and Sweet Emporium is a comfortable and entertaining stop for all. The open fire in the back room helps create a comfortable atmosphere amongst the mismatched wooden furniture and friendly service.

CONTACT
54 High Street
BD23 3LX
01756 749250

Abbey Tea Rooms

CAFÉS & TEA ROOMS | SKIPTON | BD23 6HB

Popular with walkers and cyclists, the Abbey Tearooms in Bolton Abbey offers a wide selection of hot and cold snacks and drinks. A great place to rest with a coffee after touring the Abbey, the Tearooms has a surprising array of generously portioned specials, along with their regular features.

Easy to miss, this simple and traditional tearoom will surprise you with its standards and quality. The building was once the old forge and has since been carefully transformed. The Abbey Tearoom is a popular place to enjoy refreshment close to the stunning ruins of Bolton Abbey.

CONTACT

Ferry House, Bolton Abbey
BD23 6HB
01756 710797

Annie & Betty's Tea Room

CAFÉS & TEA ROOMS | GRASSINGTON | BD23 5AQ

Located in the scenic town of Grassington, this charming tea room was named after the owner's Grandma and Great Grandma. The tearoom represents a traditional style of baking, ensuring the cakes are fresh, decadent and delicious. The interior is quaint, with lots of vintage floral and pastel shades.

The 1950s style theme is evident everywhere at Annie and Betty's Tea Room, from the china cups and saucers to the waitresses' costumes. Soft pink-hued macaroons and warm scones are piled high on cake stands in the tearoom and vintage inspired handcrafted gifts highlight the shelves in the shop.

CONTACT

7 The Square
BD23 5AQ
01756 753583

Baldersons

CAFÉS & TEA ROOMS | THORNTON LE DALE | YO18 7RW

Baldersons is a traditional bakery and sandwich bar in Thornton le Dale which has been family run since 1895. Family recipes passed down through the generations create all of the featured food, made with local ingredients, which is served in the cafe and bakery.

English breakfasts are served before noon and local favourites include their traditional hot pasties, pork pies and breakfast pastries. Baldersons Tea Garden is open all year long with a play area for children. They encourage cyclists to visit with space to leave their bikes outside, whilst they take a break from their routes.

CONTACT
Chestnut Avenue
YO18 7RW
01751 474272

Be a Garden Maker

CAFÉS & TEA ROOMS | SKIPTON | BD23 4SN

Be a Garden Maker is a bustling garden centre and tearoom in the market town of Skipton. UK grown plants are paired with unusual garden ornaments and furniture alongside their cafe. The Nectar Cafe has a huge vaulted ceiling with beautiful beams and a woodburner, making it the ideal spot for coffee and a full English breakfast or a bowl of their homemade soup for lunch.

Be a Garden Maker also has a popular reclamation business with their barns piled high with interesting and distinctive finds, from Yorkshire Stone and sundials to birdbaths.

CONTACT

Coars Farm, Wigglesworth
BD23 4SN
01729 840848

The Cinder Trail at Whitby

BY DENNIS PLATTS

Betty's Cafe Tea Rooms

CAFÉS & TEA ROOMS | HARROGATE | HG1 2QU

Betty's Cafe and Tearoom in Harrogate opened in 1919 and has retained its popularity as one of England's finest traditional tearooms. Founded by Frederick Belmont, a Swiss baker and confectioner who came to England in search of opportunities to develop his craft skills, the cafe and tearoom is still owned by the same family today.

With a focus on quality, presentation and warm Yorkshire hospitality, Betty's menu is seasonal, with fresh ingredients sourced locally from Yorkshire growers and dishes which range from regional favourites to traditional Swiss specialities, in respect of Betty's cultural heritage.

CONTACT
1 Parliament Street
HG1 2QU
01423 814070

Bloomfield Square

CAFÉS & TEA ROOMS | OTLEY | LS21 1BR

Situated in the market town of Otley, Bloomfield Square is a very popular cafe renowned for its excellent tea, coffee and home-baked cakes. The decor cleverly fuses the old Yorkshire facade, original beams, stone and wooden floors with a contemporary interior of pendant bulb lighting, a wood clad coffee bar and industrial style metal stools.

The laid back atmosphere at Bloomfield Square is evident as soon as you enter the cafe. A wood burner and sprinkling of fairy lights also create a comfortable and cozy ambience. The menu is small and considered with sandwiches being a popular option.

CONTACT

28-30 Gay Lane
LS21 1BR

Firebox Café

CAFÉS & TEA ROOMS | HAWES | DL8 3NT

Situated in the Yorkshire Dales National Park Visitor's Centre in Hawes, the Firebox Café, is part of Stage 1 Cycles, making it an ideal stop on your travels across the Dales. The Café has great coffee and prides itself on its selection of homemade cakes. A bike equipment shop and workshop is also on site.

Welcoming all, not just cyclists, the café is a much-needed oasis, providing respite from long walks and rides. Situated in the pretty old train station in Hawes, Firebox has adhered to its cycling theme with bikes suspended from the ceiling and the beautiful arched window overlooking the old trains and rails.

CONTACT

Station Yard, Burtesette Road
DL8 3NT
01969 666873

Four Corners Canteen

CAFÉS & TEA ROOMS | SHEFFIELD | S7 1FH

Inspired by global street food, Four Corners Canteen brings casual, high quality and international cuisine to Sheffield. Run by two friends and conceptualised whilst travelling, the laid back environment and rustic interior set the scene for a menu which takes you to all four corners of the world.

Breakfasts can include California's Big Sur with eggs, avocado, streaky bacon and buttermilk pancakes whilst other dishes are inspired by South African, Vietnamese, Creole and Cajun cuisine. Quality is important to the founders and artisan world teas and single origin coffee are also available.

CONTACT

150 Abbeydale Road
S7 1FH
0114 250 0768

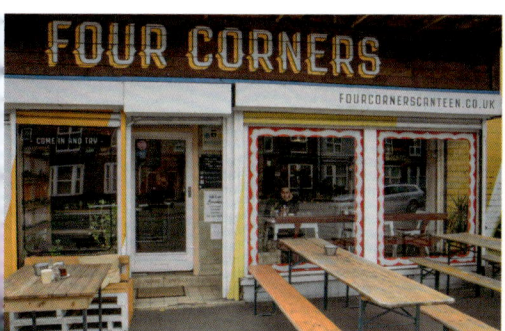

Mrs Atha's

CAFÉS & TEA ROOMS | LEEDS | LS1 6DE

Mrs Atha's in Leeds describes itself as an 'independent family run coffee shop with an emphasis on good produce and traceable provenance'. This is a beautifully designed coffee and tea house offering breakfast and lunch menus alongside its indulgent home-baked cakes, which are displayed on a sculpted wood counter.

High ceilings, brick interior walls, stripped wooden floors, industrial pendant lighting and black boards create a stylish interior reminiscent of a Brooklyn coffee house in New York. This independent cafe roasts its own coffee beans and is becoming renowned in the city for its excellence.

CONTACT
Central Road
LS1 6DE
01132 455515

Oscar's Café & Wine Bar

CAFÉS & TEA ROOMS | HOLMFIRTH | HD9 2DL

Oscar's in Holmfirth is a contemporary cafe and wine bar offering coffee and cake by day and platters, cheeseboards, antipasti and charcuterie alongside wine and cocktails in the evening. They wish to provide their guests with a 'relaxed, modern environment for people to enjoy some of the finer things in life'.

Inside Oscar's Cafe and Wine Bar you will find a contemporary, country chic aesthetic with inky blue and white walls and coffee coloured leather banquette seating. Freshly made cakes are displayed on the bar's counter and metal bar stools provide window seating to watch the world go by.

CONTACT
1 Rotcher Road
HD9 2DL
01484 767972

Saltaire Salts Mill

BRADFORD, YORKSHIRE

Pom Kitchen

CAFÉS & TEA ROOMS | SHEFFIELD | S11 8ZP

Pom is a stylish vegetarian and vegan cafe serving delicious, healthy, vibrant food in a calming environment. Wellness is the key and only clean, natural food and drink is served. A pink neon sign stating 'wild things run free' features on the white walls and lush green plants enhance the natural inspiration.

The simplicity of the interior at Pom is offset against their highly instagrammable rainbow salads and delicious array of vegetables and hearty soups. Thai curries and North African stews are filling whilst creamy vegan porridge and colourful, abundant breakfast bowls are lavishly decorated with flowers.

CONTACT
388 Sharrow Vale Road
S11 8ZP

Retreat Tearoom & Bistro

CAFÉS & TEA ROOMS | GRASSINGTON | BD23 5AA

The Retreat Tearoom and Bistro is a popular vegetarian and vegan café in the heart of Grassington, sourcing local ingredients wherever possible. In the evenings the café transforms itself into a relaxed and bustling bistro, with friendly staff, relaxing music and a great menu inspired by the chef's extensive travels.

The Retreat Tearoom and Bistro is an oasis for non-meat eaters. Alongside dishes such as vegetarian Shepherdess Pie and a Gourmet Burger, they even have dairy-free ice cream and gluten-free options. The wine menu is carefully selected and extensive.

CONTACT
14-16 Main Street
BD23 5AA
01756 751887

Scarlett's Vintage Tea Rooms

CAFÉS & TEA ROOMS | **KNARESBOROUGH** | **HG5 8AU**

Scarlett's Vintage Cafe is a quintessentially English tea room situated in a cobbled courtyard in the village of Knaresborough. Family friendly with toys, games, dolls houses and books available to play with and read, the cafe is decorated with bunting and 1940s inspired decor.

Cream teas, coffees, cakes, soups and sandwiches are the focus of the menu, with child-sized portions available. Vintage tea cups and saucers serve traditional Yorkshire tea in this old-fashioned cafe, with its white washed stone interior walls, wooden beams and pastel painted furniture.

CONTACT

3a Green Dragon Yard
HG5 8AU
07852 123139

Tea on the Green

CAFÉS & TEA ROOMS | SKIPTON | BD23 6EX

Tea on the Green is a contemporary tearoom in Bolton Abbey. Quality is the focus and everything is made attentively to order from their freshly baked cakes and scones to their sandwiches. Their "Field to fork" philosophy ensures that they use the best local ingredients, from their beef to their pies.

The beautiful setting and friendly staff add to the convivial feel and you'll be welcomed throughout the day. The Abbey estate is a great place for a walk before visiting Tea on the Green and their pretty garden, scattered with pots of flowers and hanging baskets, provides a relaxing atmosphere for all.

CONTACT

Bolton Abbey
BD23 6EX
01756 711834

The Hedgerow

CAFÉS | THRESHFIELD | BD23 5BP

The Hedgerow is a luxurious florist, gift and coffee shop in the village of Threshfield. Gifts are carefully selected from all over the world, from local artisans to ethically sourced companies, whilst flowers arrive fresh from Holland daily. A flower school on site provides courses for budding florists.

The Old School Tea Room

CAFÉS | GRASSINGTON | BD23 5DX

The Old School Tea Room has been lovingly converted from the old village school. The interior enjoys the school house's high ceilings and Victorian style windows which allow the sun to flood in. The quaint surroundings are light with white walls, wooden flooring, bunting and vintage china highlighting the room.

The Station, Richmond

CAFÉS | RICHMOND | DL10 4LD

The Station is a hub of activity and arts for both visitors and locals in Richmond. Independent retailers, a contemporary café/bar, a three screen cinema, a brewery and exhibition spaces are all located in this transformed former Victorian railway station. Weekly workshops and events are also held on site such as yoga and singing.

The Tea Cottage

CAFÉS | SKIPTON | BD23 6EX

The Tea Cottage is a fine English tearoom in Bolton Abbey providing home-cooked food and afternoon-teas in an idyllic cottage setting. Farmhouse furniture, open fires and original stone windows create a quintessentially English ambience whilst mouth-watering cakes are displayed on stands under the traditional oak beams.

The Whippet & Pickle

CAFÉS | **HOLMFIRTH** | **HD9 1HA**

The Whippet & Pickle say that their ethos is 'tasty, affordable & honest cooking using the freshest produce, homemade and as local as possible'. This contemporary restaurant and cinema offers a considered menu from breakfast through to dinner with a seasonal influence and an emphasis on quality.

The Wrinkled Stocking

CAFÉS | **HOLMFIRTH** | **HD9 2JS**

The Wrinkled Stocking Tearoom is a vintage tearoom situated in Holmfirth. You step back in time as soon as you enter this friendly establishment, where dogs are also welcomed. Floral print pastel wallpaper, white lace bunting and floral china only add to the vintage appeal of this popular tearoom.

Walkers Bakers

CAFÉS | **SKIPTON** | **BD23 1PB**

This family-run business was set up with the aim of providing locals and visitors with the best breads, cakes and pastries, using the finest ingredients. Robert Walker is still the hands-on baker, but has expanded to open bakeries in nearby towns too. He's kept busy creating and developing new and original treats for his customers.

York Cocoa House

CAFÉS | **YORK** | **YO1 8QJ**

The York Cocoa House is a chocolate emporium, cafe and haven for chocolate lovers with hand-made chocolates and chocolate workshops available. With an interior resembling a old world chocolatier lifted straight out of a traditional French village, the Cocoa House exudes the owner's passion for everything related to chocolate.

FOOD
SHOPS

YORKSHIRE

Cheese & Wine Emporium

FOOD SHOPS | YORK | YO1 8AS

The Cheese & Wine Emporium, situated on Stonegate in a Grade II listed building, is one of the Cheshire Cheese Company's retail stores. Having won international awards for its produce, their interesting cheese flavours and combinations include Caramelised Onion & Rioja and their spicy El Gringo Chilli, Lime & Tequila Cheddar.

The traditional store interior is rustic with samples of their cheeses available to taste each day. A wide selection of crackers and chutneys are also available alongside their extensive wine collection, which offers affordable boutique vineyard wines from all over the world.

CONTACT

6 Stonegate
YO1 8AS
0808 189 0725

Henshelwoods Delicatessen

FOOD SHOPS | YORK | YO1 7LA

Henshelwoods Delicatessen is an authentic deli in the heart of York overlooking the daily market, from which they source the finest and freshest local and seasonal produce. Priding themselves upon their exquisite local ingredients, they also source delicacies from around the world.

At Henshelwoods Deli, homemade terrines, soups, salads and sweet tarts are sold. With old-fashioned values, the deli stocks an extensive range of British and continental cheeses, olives, charcuterie, condiments and locally made spirits and beers. Hampers are popular with customers and can be made bespoke to your requirements.

CONTACT

10 New Street
YO1 7LA
01904 673877

Stanforth Butchers

FOOD SHOPS | SKIPTON | BD23 1NJ

At Stanforth Butchers, the queue regularly goes around the block for possibly the best pork pies in Yorkshire. Established over 80 years ago, this unassuming, traditional pie emporium remains incredibly popular, due to their outstanding quality.

Using traditional methods and the finest locally sourced ingredients, they have kept to the time-honoured recipes that their customers expect. Their pork, lamb and beef cuts are fresh and bought directly from the market, and animal welfare is paramount. This is the place to buy cooked and uncooked meat in the Skipton area.

CONTACT

9-11 Mill Bridge
BD23 1NJ
01756 793477

The Angel's Share Bakery

FOOD SHOPS | RICHMOND | DL10 4LD

The Angel's Share Bakery is a truly artisanal bakery with a focus on crafting the very best of breads and patisserie, using family recipes passed down through the generations alongside newly developed recipes. They produce four/five varieties of bread daily, using a variety of British, French and Yorkshire flours.

As finalists on Britain's Best Bakery on ITV, The Angel's Share Bakery is now nationally renowned. Situated in the recently converted Old Station building in Richmond, both their bakery and store offer a contemporary environment to showcase their delicious creations, including the popular 'Lancer Loaf'.

CONTACT
Richmond Station, Station Yard
DL10 4LD
01748 828261

The Courtyard Dairy

FOOD SHOPS | AUSTWICK | LA2 8AS

The Courtyard Dairy is a characterful and expert cheesemongers selling the best artisanal cheeses from Britain and around the world. Regularly featuring in the national press and having won numerous awards for its excellence, The Courtyard Dairy is renowned for its quality produce and knowledgeable staff.

The Courtyard Dairy sells condiments and wines to accompany their extensive collection of cheeses. From their cheese club and hampers to their spectacular cheese wedding cakes, The Courtyard Dairy's passion for their produce is palpable from the moment you walk through the door of their beautiful stone barn.

CONTACT

Crows Nest Barn
LA2 8AS
01729 823 291

Ribblehead Viaduct

CARNFORTH, NORTH YORKSHIRE

The Farm Shop at Cannon Hall

FOOD SHOPS | CAWTHORNE | S75 4AT

Famous for its fine, home produced beef, pork and lamb, Cannon Hall Farm Shop has twice been a finalist in the White Rose Awards "Taste of Yorkshire" competition. With a traditional approach to service and quality, the farm shop uses their own meat created from traditional farming and butchery methods, handed down through the generations.

Sourcing the highest quality produce from all over Yorkshire, Cannon Hall Farm shop also has its own bakery, producing award winning pies, cakes and artisan bread. Their small pork pie was voted runner up in the prestigious Yorkshire Pork Pie and Sausage Championship 2014.

CONTACT

Bark House Lane
S75 4AT
01226 792746

The Oldest Sweetshop in England

FOOD SHOPS | PATELEY BRIDGE | HG3 5JZ

The Oldest Sweetshop in England, as verified by the Guinness Book of Records, has traded since 1827. The shop has featured on numerous TV programmes and their knowledge of and passion for traditional sweets and sweet making is second to none.

The Oldest Sweetshop in England prides itself upon old-fashioned quality from its confectionery and shop aesthetic to its customer service. As one of the few remaining traditional sweet shops in the country, this store is authentic in every respect. Its fantastic array of sweets, jars and chocolate can now be sold worldwide, thanks to their online business.

CONTACT

39 High Street
HG3 5JZ
01423 712371

The Whitby Deli

FOOD SHOPS | **WHITBY** | **YO21 3BA**

The Whitby Deli kitchen puts an emphasis on serving local produce from their seasonal menu, which features daily specials. Their vibrant dining area is accessorised with pops of sunshine yellow and turquoise and offers the perfect environment to have what they claim to be, the best coffee in town.

At The Whitby Deli they stock the best of Yorkshire's produce, with their shelves packed high with award-winning own-label chutneys, jams and preserves alongside sweet and savoury treats and artisan chocolates. The deli offers a fantastic range of vegetarian and Gluten Free produce including pâté, cakes and pasta.

CONTACT

22-23 Flowergate
YO21 3BA
01947 229062

Vanessa Delicatessen & Café

FOOD SHOPS | BEVERLEY | HU17 8BB

Passionate about supplying the highest quality, local produce by supporting local farmers, Vanessa Delicatessen and café currently stocks over thirty local farmers' produce, with an aim to continue expanding this list.

The Vanessa café provides seasonal, local ingredients in their popular dishes, which can be bought individually from the delicatessen once you have sampled them. The cafe and deli are modern and have a farm shop ambience, with their fridge counters overflowing with antipasti, cheeses, pies and freshly baked cakes and scones.

CONTACT

21-22 Saturday Market
HU17 8BB
01482 868190

Wensleydale Creamery

FOOD SHOPS | HAWES | DL8 3RN

Wensleydale Creamery produces the real Wensleydale cheese, one of the UK's best-loved and best-known cheeses. The proudly independent Creamery includes a museum detailing the thousand-year history of the cheese and a visitor centre where you can learn (some) of the secrets of cheese-making as well as doing cheese tastings.

Important for employment, tourism and supplying local produce, The Wensleydale Creamery produces 4,000 tonnes of cheese a year, using traditional methods. Based in Hawes, in the heart of the Yorkshire Dales, the creamery has a well-stocked shop selling the cheesemaker's celebrated produce.

CONTACT

Gayle Lane
DL8 3RN
01969 667664

Wilfred Deli

FOOD SHOPS | **RICHMOND** | DL10 4QA

The Wilfred Deli & Pantry is a beautifully refined and contemporary deli in Richmond offering a carefully curated collection of quality wines, cheeses, condiments and olive oils. Simple, seasonal food is served here with an emphasis on the calibre of the ingredients.

Delicious coffees and teas are served alongside their flavoursome cakes, of which their orange and almond is a favourite. Olives, freshly baked ciabatta bread and sausage rolls all regularly feature on the menu. Dark polished wood flooring, bright white walls and high ceilings make The Wilfred Deli a stylish choice for breakfast or lunch.

CONTACT

13a Finkle Street
DL10 4QA
01748 821034

North Landing Flamborough

BY SUE SLATER

BEST OF ENGLAND

SMITHY
ENTRANCE
EASE LEAVE CLEAR
AT ALL TIMES

CULTURE & HISTORY

YORKSHIRE

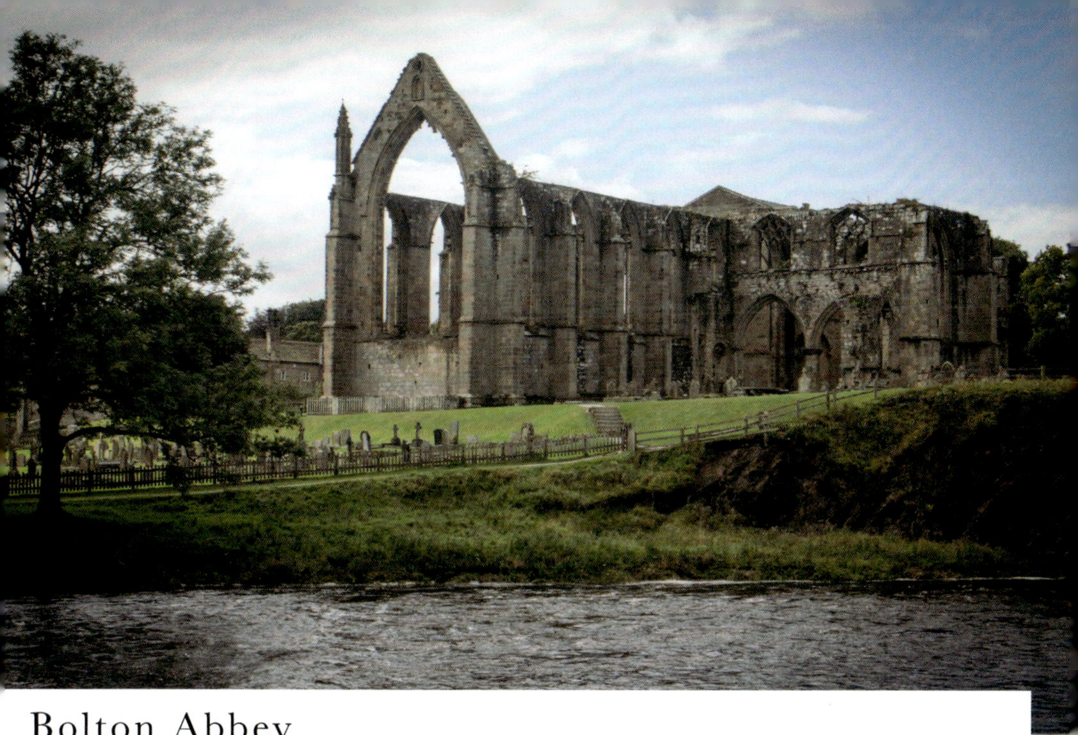

Bolton Abbey

CULTURE | **SKIPTON** | BD23 6AL

Bolton Abbey Estate is a great day out for all the family. There are a number of walks around the estate, which take in everything from the fascinating Priory Church and Ruins to tumbling waterfalls and even stepping-stones over a large expanse of river. The walks primarily run along the river and through attractive woodland.

Along the walking trails are countless eateries and places of interest, and if you want to fully treat yourself, you can dine at the 4 AA Rosette Burlington Restaurant within the Devonshire Arms Hotel & Spa. Parking varies in price throughout the year, but is well worth it.

CONTACT

Bolton Abbey
BD23 6AL
01756 718 000

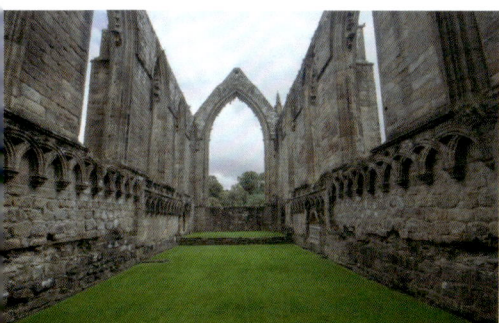

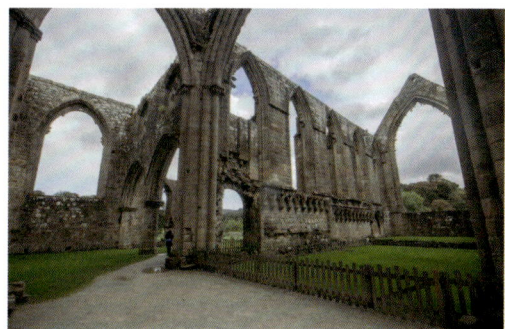

Cannon Hall

CULTURE | **CAWTHORNE** | S75 4AT

Set within 70 acres of historic parkland and an attractive landscaped garden is Cannon Hall Museum, near Cawthorne. Inside the museum, there are an interesting mix of paintings, ceramics, modern glassware and furniture collections displayed in historic rooms.

Outside in the park is the historic walled garden, with an extensive pear collection, a magnificent greenhouse, the remains of a pinery – which was used to grow exotic fruits, and fairyland, a whimsical garden with arches and pillars. Cannon Hall is free to visit and interesting for all ages.

CONTACT

Bark House Lane
S75 4AT
01226 772 002

Dales Countryside Museum

CULTURE | HAWES | DL8 3NT

The Dales Countryside Museum covers how the landscape, wildlife and people of this stunning area of natural beauty have changed and evolved from prehistoric times until today. It's housed in the disused Hawes railway station and part of the museum includes a real steam train and carriages of former transportation.

In addition to its displays of objects and wealth of information, the museum hosts temporary exhibitions, events and activities. The collection focuses on the social and industrial history of the area and each item has its own intriguing story.

CONTACT

Station Yard, Burtersett Road
DL8 3NT
01969 666210

Georgian Theatre Royal

CULTURE | **RICHMOND** | DL10 4DW

The Georgian Theatre Royal in Richmond was built in 1788 and is Britain's most complete Georgian playhouse and Britain's oldest working theatre in its original form. Today it's a thriving community playhouse and living theatre museum. The auditorium has a capacity of 214 places in a close, intimate proximity to the stage and nightly performances include everything from plays and comedy to unique music.

For a small fee you can view behind-the-scenes with the theatre's hourly tours, which give you a unique insight into the history of the theatre. The theatre is also home to Britain's oldest surviving stage scenery.

CONTACT
Victoria Road
DL10 4DW
01748 823710

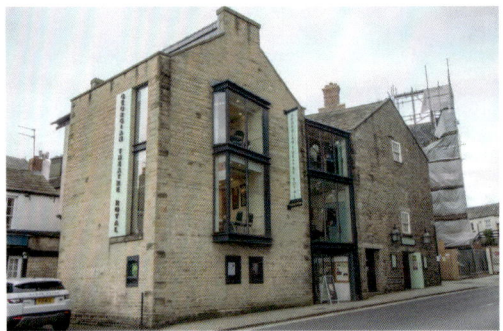

Green Howards Museum

CULTURE | **RICHMOND** | DL10 4QN

The Green Howards Museum is a unique collection of military artifacts and personal items with a connection to the Green Howards Regiment, Yorkshire's infantry regiment of the British Army. The collection started in the years following the First World War and has steadily grown.

The collection is home to more than 35,000 objects and includes over 200 uniforms, 4000 medals, an array of weaponry including machine guns, revolvers and swords as well as historical personal photographs, documents and memorabilia. The Green Howards Museum is located in the center of Richmond.

CONTACT
19 Church Wynd
DL10 4QN
01748 826561

Leeds City Museum

CULTURE | **LEEDS** | **LS2 8BH**

Leeds City Museum is located on Millennium Square in the centre of the city and is an educational museum with natural history displays, artwork and historical exhibitions about Leeds. The Museum has many interactive items too, making learning fun for children.

The Museum is completely free for visitors and on-site there is also a shop and café selling light refreshments. Highlights include the Roman floor mosaic circa 250 CE, the Leeds mummy thought to be 3000 years old and a Hellenistic Greek tomb ca 250 BC.

CONTACT

Millennium Square
LS2 8BH
01132 243732

Nidderdale Museum

CULTURE | **PATELEY BRIDGE** | **HG3 5LE**

Nidderdale's Local History Museum is set over eleven separate rooms, which illustrate distinct aspects of Nidderdale life through the ages. The rooms include exhibits devoted to leisure, agriculture, transport, costume and more. There are also scene rooms that recreate spaces such as an original cobblers shop, schoolroom, general store and Victorian parlour room.

The museum has won multiple awards. The idea originated from a group of enthusiasts who shared a deep concern that traditional ways of living were rapidly disappearing so they decided to preserve a slice of history in an educational way.

CONTACT

The Old Workhouse, King Street
HG3 5LE
01423 711225

Richmond Castle

CULTURE | RICHMOND | DL10 4QW

Richmond Castle is a great Norman fortress situated above the cliff-lined valley of the river Swale. Much of the original curtain wall of the castle remains in place today together with many of the castle's main buildings.

The castle has a fascinating history and some impressive structures to help you recreate an image of its past. The keep is 30 meters tall and is thought to be from the mid-12th century. You can climb to the top of the keep for excellent views over the castle and Richmond. Another highlight is the contemporary Cockpit Garden with ornamental flowerbeds, paths and the remains of a glasshouse.

CONTACT

Tower Street
DL10 4QW
0370 333 1181

Ripon Cathedral

CULTURE | RIPON | HG4 1QT

A stone church has occupied the site on which the grand Ripon Cathedral sits, since the year 672. Although it has been rebuilt and built upon since, within certain areas of the church including the choir and the nave you can see evidence of 800 years worth of craftsmanship in the wood and stone.

Spectacular features such as the organ, the rood screen, misericords and crypt are certainly worth seeking out. Also noteworthy is the church's own choir, who sing at six services a week. Try and visit during a service to appreciate the acoustics and ambience in full.

CONTACT

Minster Road
HG4 1QT
01765 603462

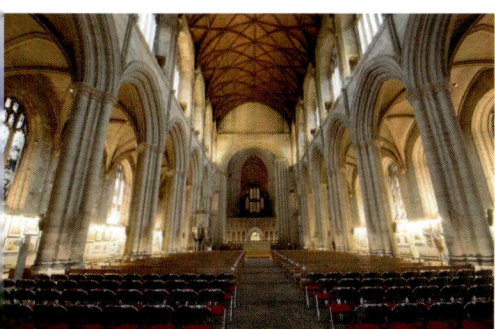
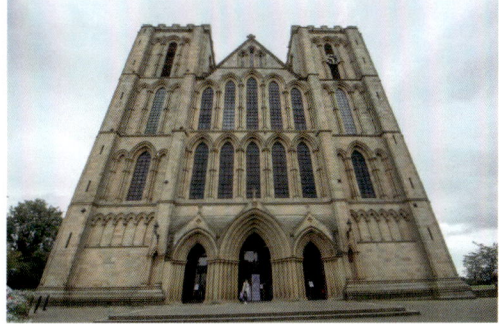

Sheffield Botanical Gardens

CULTURE | SHEFFIELD | S10 2LN

Sheffield Botanical Gardens showcase 5,000 species of plants over 19 acres of landscaped gardens. They were first opened in 1836 and have since been a place of relaxation and beauty for the people of Sheffield and its visitors. Entrance to the gardens is free and onsite is the Curator's House Restaurant and Tea Rooms.

Throughout the year there are a number of different events including music in the gardens, theatre productions and storytelling. The Victorian glasshouse is particularly attractive and well worth a visit. The gardens are a great escape from the busy city and are open year-round.

CONTACT

Clarkehouse Road
S10 2LN
0114 268 6001

The Brontë Parsonage Museum

CULTURE | HAWORTH | BD22 8DR

The Brontë Parsonage Museum is the original home of the Brontë family, where renowned novelists Emily, Anne and Charlotte grew up. The surrounding North Yorkshire countryside proved to be the perfect inspiration for the sisters as from there they wrote classics such as 'Wuthering Heights', 'Jane Eyre' and 'The Tenant of Wildfell Hall".

The Brontë Society is one of the oldest literary societies in the world and runs the museum, which houses the largest collection of manuscripts written by the sisters. Visiting the museum offers a unique insight into the Brontës' life and upbringing.

CONTACT

Church Street
BD22 8DR
01535 642323

The View to Cayton Bay

BY CHRISTOPHER NAYLOR

The Henry Moore Institute

CULTURE | **LEEDS** | LS1 3AH

The Henry Moore Institute is an international research centre and exhibition space in Leeds. The Museum is dedicated to celebrating sculpture, where famed sculptor Henry Moore began his training. They host a varied programme of exhibitions and events and are home to an invaluable sculpture research library.

The Henry Moore Institute is free to visit and is a must for those interested in the arts. The building itself is unique and visually impressive. You can also visit the collections, which are housed in the adjacent Leeds Art Gallery building accessed via a bridge link from the institute.

CONTACT

74 The Headrow
LS1 3AH
01132 467467

The Old Grammar School

CULTURE | OTLEY | LS21 3AY

The Old Grammar School Gallery is an intriguing and inspiring space and has become a landmark in the centre of Otley. The building is worth a visit itself, and the gallery's regularly changing exhibitions showcase the wide variety of local artistic talent using different mediums.

Burtersett Studio

CULTURE | HAWES | DL8 3NP

Burtersett Studio and Gallery in Hawes, North Yorkshire, features many watercolours, oil paintings and other fine art with local flavour. The intriguing recent works of Brian Alderman, who moved to the area from Scotland, show his fascination with all things Dales-related.

Werxzovart

CULTURE | HAWORTH | BD22 8DA

Werxzovart is ceramic artist Sonje Hibbert's gallery in which she showcases her best works. She takes her inspiration from nature and the surroundings in which she lives and visits and this is evident in her creations. Her original designs have been influenced by many years travelling throughout Asia and the UK and often include humour.

York Castle

CULTURE | YORK | YO1 9SA

A visit to York Castle's Clifford's Tower, gives you the opportunity to scale the steep steps of the ancient mound and tour the tower. The remains of this Medieval Norman castle are the ruins of its fortified tower and 'keep'. From the wall you can see the 18th century buildings, which form the eye of York and serve as the York Castle Museum and Crown Court.

York Minster

CULTURE | YORK | YO1 7HH

York Minster is one of the world's most spectacular cathedrals, with its delightful stained glass windows, historic artefacts, incredible architecture and history. For a further £5 you can climb the 275 winding steps for unsurpassable views over York and the medieval pinnacles of the Minster's towers.

York River Walk

CULTURE | YORK | YO1 7DR

The River Ouse runs through York and is a wonderful way to see the city without being overwhelmed by tourists. The Eastern part of the river is lined with plenty of restaurants and cafes, perfect for refreshments, yet there are multiple spots of lush grass to enjoy a picnic whilst watching the boats and ducks in the sun.

Yorkshire Museum

CULTURE | YORK | YO1 7FR

The Yorkshire Museum has been exhibiting collections for close to 200 years and is one of the earliest purpose-built museums in the country. The Museum houses five galleries showcasing fascinating archaeological treasures and many rare animals, birds and fossils in themed displays.

Yorkshire Sculpture Park

CULTURE | WEST BRETTON | WF4 4JX

The Yorkshire Sculpture Park is situated in the 500-acre, 18th century Bretton Hall Estate and is the largest of its kind in Europe. More than 80 works are on display across the site. The sculptures include bronzes by Henry Moore, Barbara Hepworth's "The Family of Man" and site-specific works by David Nash, Andy Goldsworthy and other world-leading artists.

Whitby Abbey

CULTURE | **WHITBY** | YO22 4JT

Perched on Whitby's East Cliff, overlooking the North Sea are the remains of Gothic Whitby Abbey. The first monastery on the site was founded in 657, which became one of the most important religious centers in the Anglo-Saxon world. To get to the Abbey you can count the 199 steps to the top of the headland from the town.

Back in 1890, the author Bram Stoker drew inspiration from the ruins and it assisted him with creating the renowned novel Dracula. The remains here still captivate visitors with the interesting architecture and stunning views overlooking the sea and Whitby town.

CONTACT

Abbey Lane
YO22 4JT
0370 333 1181

BEST OF ENGLAND

PLACES TO VISIT

LAKE DISTRICT

Ambleside

PLACES TO VISIT | AMBLESIDE | LA22 9AN

Ambleside has a rich Roman history, with a fort named Galava, dating from AD79 and situated just south of the town. Today it serves as a base for those exploring the surrounding countryside and is particularly popular with climbers, hikers and mountain bikers.

Situated at the head of Lake Windemere, England's largest natural lake, Ambleside offers pubs, hotels, restaurants and shops, as well as boat trips across the water to soak up the mesmerising views. The outdoor interests of those that visit Ambleside is evident in the multitude of shops catering to climbing and biking needs.

CONTACT

1-3 Rydal Road
LA22 9AN

Bassenthwaite Lake

PLACES TO VISIT | KESWICK | CA13 9YD

Bassenthwaite Lake is one of the largest lakes in this region. Owned by the National Park Authority, the lake remains unspoilt with very little development on its shores. A small open-air theatre was built here in 1974, where it is thought that the poet Tennyson composed much of his poem 'Morte D'Arthur'.

Bassenthwaite Lake is a popular spot for sailing, with a boat club situated on its banks. A lakeside path on the western side offers beautiful views over the shimmering water. A wetland nature reserve is situated in the northern region of the lake, which is known for its rare birds and fish.

CONTACT

Lakeside
CA13 9YD

Bowness-on-Windermere

PLACES TO VISIT | WINDERMERE | LA23 3HQ

Situated on the shore of Lake Windermere, Bowness-on-Windermere is one of the most popular tourist destinations in the Lake District due to it being a centre for outdoor and adventure activities. From a humble fishing village to a vibrant tourist destination, a number of the hotels today have been converted from large Victorian residences.

The Lake District's spectacular beauty and abundant wildlife inspired Beatrix Potter to write her much-loved stories. At Bowness-on-Windermere her tales are brought to life in the interactive 'World of Beatrix Potter,' a museum dedicated to the author.

CONTACT

Bowness-on-Windermere
LA23 3HQ

Blea Tarn in Langdale, Lake District

BY FRANCIS VALLELY

Brougham Castle

PLACES TO VISIT | PENRITH | CA10 2AA

Dating back to the 13th century, the imposing ruins of Brougham Castle are situated near the picturesque crossing of the River Eamont in Cumbria. Known by its impressive double gatehouse and tower, the castle is an impressive and historically rich English Heritage site.

Built as a protective barrier against Scots invaders and as a respected residence, Brougham Castle fell into disrepair in the 1600s. However, even in its dilapidated condition, it remains an impressive landmark on the river Eamont. Panoramic views over the Eden Valley can be seen from the top of the castle's keep.

CONTACT

Moor Lane
CA10 2AA
01768 862488

Buttermere

PLACES TO VISIT | COCKERMOUTH | CA13 9XA

Buttermere is surrounded by vertiginous mountains and tranquil countryside. The path that runs the perimeter of Buttermere Lake can be completed within two to three hours and is popular with families. Owned by The National Trust, Buttermere Lake is renowned for its natural beauty and its name means 'lake by the dairy pastures'.

Buttermere Lake offers true serenity. With just a few farms and a couple of inns and cafés, the area remains rural and picturesque. Nearby, Syke Farm has a tearoom and is known for its homemade ice cream, made from the milk of its own herd of Ayrshire cattle.

CONTACT

Buttermere
CA13 9XA

Cartmel

PLACES TO VISIT | CARTMEL | LA11 6QB

The South Lakeland District fells and countryside surround Cartmel and its famous 12th Century medieval Priory Church offers centuries of enthralling history. The village itself offers great food and dining opportunities from artisan bread and cheese shops to traditional pubs.

Rich in culture and heritage, Cartmel is full of 16th-18th century buildings and the pretty river Eea streams through the village in a picturesque fashion. The village has become a haven for food lovers, from the village store's award-winning 'sticky toffee pudding' to the nationally acclaimed, Michelin starred restaurant L'Enclume.

CONTACT

The Square, Cavendish Street
LA11 6QB

Coniston

PLACES TO VISIT | CONISTON | LA21 8DU

Coniston was historically famous for its ore and slate mining. During Victorian times, the Furness Railway terminated in Coniston which opened up tourism to this beautiful area. Today hill-walking, rock-climbing and boating are popular pursuits from the village base.

Coniston offers a range of hotels, pubs and restaurants for those visiting the area. Grizedale Forest and Furness Fells offer walkers rugged and scenic countryside with majestic viewpoints. Tarn Hows (Tarn meaning lake), situated just a couple of miles away is a popular and beautiful spot for families to visit.

CONTACT

1 Yewdale Road
LA21 8DU
015394 41335

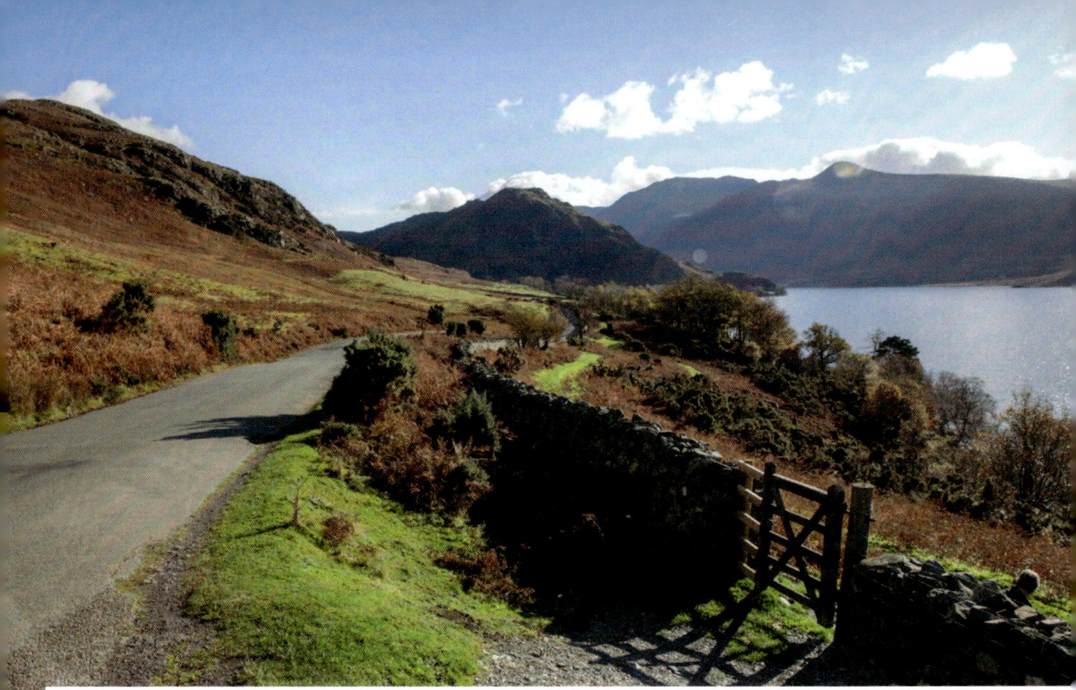

Crummock Water

PLACES TO VISIT | **COCKERMOUTH** | CA13 9UY

Walking from the car park, the woodland dramatically opens up with incredible views of Crummock Water and over Grasmor, Rannerdale Knotts, Mellbreak and Red Pike. Wild swimming is popular in this lake and the more adventurous can take the (at times challenging) nine mile walk around the lake.

During bluebell season, the valley is illuminated in a magical purple-blue haze. Across Crummock is Scale Force, the tallest single drop waterfall in the Lake District with a height of 170 feet. Several paths lead up to the waterfall. The walk there and back from Buttermere car park is around two hours.

CONTACT

B5289
CA13 9UY

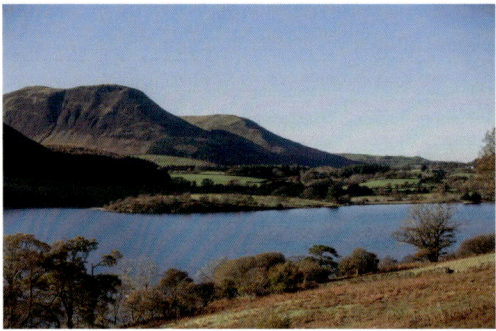

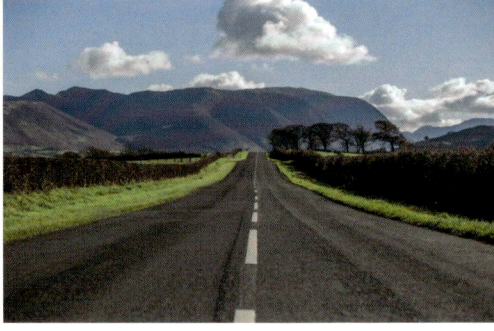

Derwentwater

PLACES TO VISIT | KESWICK | CA12 5UP

Derwentwater is where the 2016 movie Swallows and Amazons was filmed. The natural beauty and wild landscape reinforces why the original books were inspired by these enchanting surroundings. Four islands are situated in Derwentwater and canoes can be hired to create your own adventure around the lake.

The islands in Derwentwater are cared for by the National Trust and the largest, named St Herbert's, was the inspiration for the fictional Owl Island in Beatrix Potter's 'The Tale of Squirrel Nutkin'. Diverse flora and fauna inhabit the lake, so certain areas are naturally protected with no-paddle zones.

CONTACT

Borrowdale
CA12 5UP

Ford Park

PLACES TO VISIT | ULVERSTON | LA12 7JP

Ford Park is a nine-acre green space with open fields, woodland and mature gardens surrounding the Grade II listed buildings situated in Ulverston.The space is ideal if you need to give the kids a bit of a run around. Activities include a nature trail, zip wires and orienteering through the woodland.

Ford Park is also an ideal starting point to see the Sir John Barrow Monument, a 100ft high lighthouse built to honour a famous son of Ulverston. Be sure to reward yourself with a pastry or pork pie afterwards at the on site Kitchen Garden and Café.

CONTACT

Road Park
LA12 7JP
01229 580666

Grasmere

PLACES TO VISIT | GRASMERE | LA22 9SY

Situated in the centre of the Lake District, Grasmere is best known for its famous resident, the poet William Wordsworth who described it as "the loveliest spot that man hath ever found." Its enchanting beauty attracts visitors from all over the world. Today the town is a tourist destination and offers a wide range of gift shops, cafés and accommodation.

The captivating countryside which surrounds Grasmere includes fells and mountains, lush woodland and tranquil lakes. Poets, writers and painters have been inspired by this stunning landscape for generations and it only takes one visit to see why.

CONTACT

Broadgate House
LA22 9SY

Derwent Water, Keswick

BY MANDY SPEIGHT

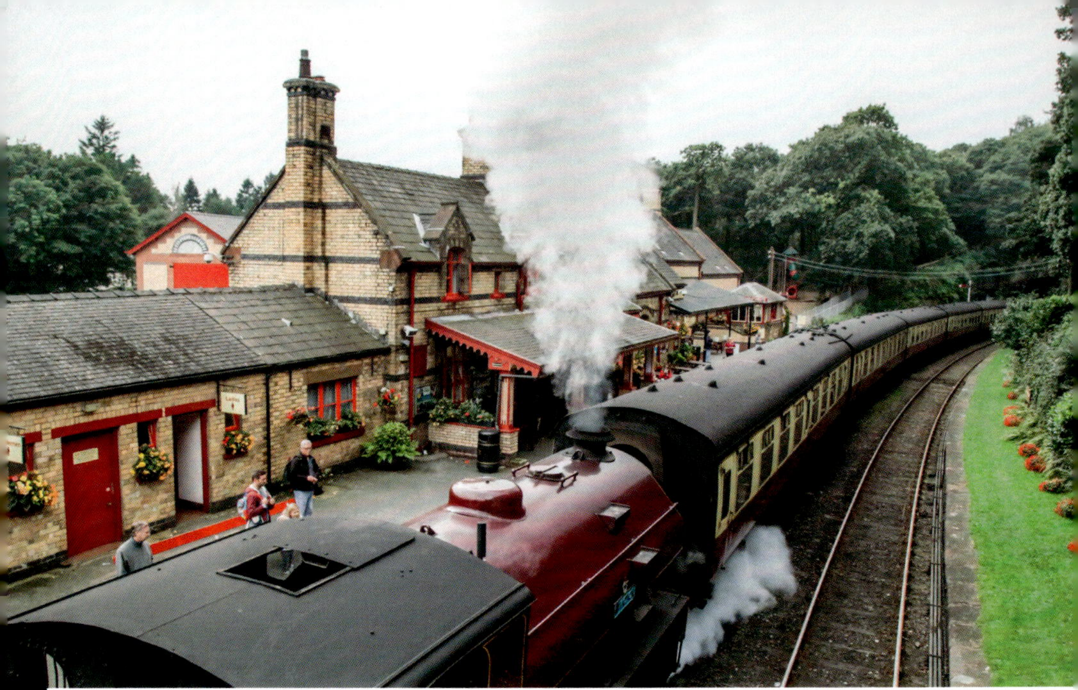

Haverthwaite Station

PLACES TO VISIT | **HAVERTHWAITE** | LA12 8AL

Visit a bygone age by climbing aboard a steam train at Haverthwaite Station and enjoy the stunning views across Lake Windermere. The Furness Railway was developed during the 1850's and 1860's, at the height of the Industrial Revolution, to transport coal and iron ore from the coastal mines to the heavy industries of the North West and North East of England.

The station provides information on the fascinating history of the railway, and a fine collection of beautiful locomotives and rolling stock. It includes a shop, restaurant, playground and an engine shed, where a fine collection of locomotives are on display.

CONTACT

Haverthwaite Station
LA12 8AL
015395 31594

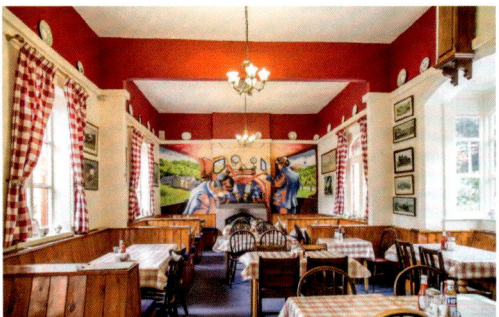

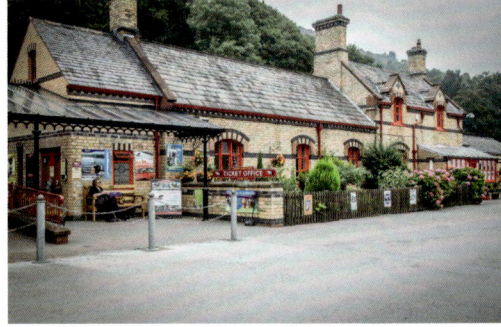

Hawkshead Brewery

PLACES TO VISIT | KENDAL | LA8 9LR

Hawkshead Brewery is a small-scale brewery that is passionate about beer. Since 2002 it has been brewing traditional English beer with a contemporary twist. The processes are hands-on, with little automation, and the brewers hand-source all their hops to create brews that are pretty special.

Hawkshead Brewery's award-winning beer hall showcases every beer they produce and is an ideal spot for a long lunch, a relaxing tasting or simply to enjoy the regular live music sessions. Here you can try the great range of beers, from the core Lakeland range and the specials to the sought-after limited editions.

CONTACT

Back Lane
LA8 9LR
01539 822644

Keswick Launch

PLACES TO VISIT | LAKESIDE | CA12 5DJ

Keswick Launch Co. offers lake cruises to experience the natural beauty of Derwentwater, with staggering views of the surrounding fells. The four launches have open and covered decks and operate on a regular timetable throughout the year. You can also explore the lake at your own pace on one of their rowing boats.

Take the 50 minute round boat trip with Keswick Launch Co. or disembark at one of their eight jetties en-route, to discover famous landmarks such as Ashness Bridge, Lodore Falls and Lingholm, the holiday home of Beatrix Potter.

CONTACT

The Waters Edge
CA12 5DJ

Kirkby Lonsdale

PLACES TO VISIT | CARNFORTH | LA6 2AE

Kirkby Lonsdale is situated on the river Lune and on the edge of the Yorkshire Dales. Popular with walkers and cyclists, the Three Peaks are close by, making it an appealing base for those touring the area. This scenic small town is full of stone-built houses and plenty of respected restaurants, pubs and hotels.

Close to the spectacular Ingleton Falls and many lush, woodland trails, Kirky Lonsdale and the surrounding Lune Valley offer a stunning and diverse landscape for walkers and visitors. The town presents many quality, independent boutiques.

CONTACT
Kirkby Lonsdale
LA6 2AE

Grasmere, Lake District

BY MARGARET VALLELY

Kirkstone Pass

PLACES TO VISIT | WINDERMERE | LA23 1PS

Kirkstone Pass has an altitude of 1,489 feet and is the Lake District's highest pass open to cars, connecting Ambleside in the Rothay Valley to Patterdale in the Ullswater valley. There are many scenic viewpoints along the pass and the 500 year old Kirkstone Pass Inn, reportedly the third highest inn in England, stands close to the summit.

Old Hall Farm

PLACES TO VISIT | BOUTH | LA12 8JA

Set in idyllic surroundings, Old Hall Farm is a great day out for the family. This working farm is run according to authentic 19th century methods, with horse power and early vintage tractors used to work the fields. They aim to retain the old techniques and the farm is almost self-sufficient in terms of feed and stock rearing.

Ravenglass Station

PLACES TO VISIT | RAVENGLASS | CA18 1SW

The Ravenglass and Eskdale Railway is one of the oldest and longest narrow gauge railways in England. The heritage steam engines still transport passengers through scenically stunning scenery from Ravenglass, the only coastal village in the Lake District National Park to Dalegarth for Boot station.

Ruskin's View

PLACES TO VISIT | CARNFORTH | LA6 2BB

The breathtaking panorama of the Lune Valley and Underley Hall can be seen from Ruskin's View. Painted by the celebrated artist JMW Turner in 1822. The 19th century art critic John Ruskin described the painting and scene as 'one of the loveliest views in England, therefore in the world'.

Rydal Water

PLACES TO VISIT | AMBLESIDE | LA22 9LW

Wordsworth's Seat at Rydal Water was reportedly the romantic poet's favourite viewpoint in the Lake District. Rydal Water is the smallest lake in the region at just 3/4 mile long and 1/4 mile wide. The landscape around the lake is fascinating and Rydal Cave, a dramatic man-made cavern in the hill above the lake, provided slate over two hundred years ago to local villagers.

St. Bees

PLACES TO VISIT | ST BEES | CA27 0ET

St Bees is well-known for its Norman Priory dating from 1120 and for being the starting point of the Wainwright "Coast to Coast" Walk. Just 50 miles South of the Scottish Border, this coastal town has a large sandy beach and has been a popular tourist destination for 150 years.

Stott Park Bobbin Mill

PLACES TO VISIT | ULVERSTON | LA12 8AX

Stott Park Bobbin Mill achieved Silver in the Small Visitor Attraction of the Year Category at the Enjoy England Awards and Gold at the Cumbria Tourism Awards. Historically this extensive working mill produced millions of wooden bobbins vital to Lancashire's spinning and weaving industries. Today it is still a working bobbin mill.

The Lakes Distillery

PLACES TO VISIT | NEAR BASSENTHWAITE LAKE | CA13 9SJ

The vision of The Lakes Distillery is to create one of the leading malt spirits in the world, alongside one of the most unique visitor experiences in the Lake District. Located in a converted Victorian cattle farm, the creation of this world-class production facility of quality spirits was a labour of love.

BEST OF ENGLAND

PUBS

LAKE DISTRICT

Fenwick Arms

PUB | **CLAUGHTON** | LA2 9LA

The beautiful Fenwick Arms is over 250 years old and exudes historic and atmospheric charm. The stylish interior cleverly incorporates the beautiful features of the old building, with its stone walls, large open fires and oak floors into a luxurious, country chic aesthetic.

Sensational seafood specials are delivered with exceptional quality at The Fenwick Arms. Daily changing specials reflect the seasonality of the menu and feature the catch of the day, straight from celebrated fishmonger Chris Neve at Fleetwood fishing port. The nine contemporary guest rooms are well appointed and elegant.

CONTACT

Lancaster Road
LA2 9LA
015242 21157

Fish Inn

PUB | COCKERMOUTH | CA13 9XA

The Fish Inn is situated next to Buttermere Lake and surrounded by the mesmerising beauty of the hills and water. Just five minutes walk from Buttermere and Crummock Water at the foot of Honister Pass, the inn is full of charm and character. Historically, this was the home of Mary Robinson (The Maid of Buttermere).

Passionate about ales, The Fish Inn sells a great selection of locally produced varieties. It is the location of the pub which attracts visitors, many of whom are walkers, soaking up the awe-inspiring beauty of the area. The menu is classic and the interior is basic and quite old-fashioned.

CONTACT

Buttermere
CA13 9XA
017687 70253

Hare and Hounds

PUB | KENDAL | LA8 8PN

The Hare and Hounds is situated in a perfect position for visiting the Lake District and is a fully refurbished coaching inn dating back to the 17th century. They provide great home-inspired meals, using local ingredients where possible. The black slate floors and open fire, create a cosy and convivial atmosphere.

Much like the styling of the pub and restaurant below, the comfy rooms are a fusion of Victorian and contemporary design. The Hare and Hounds nestles in stunning surroundings and is a welcome place to rejuvenate after a day of walking or being outdoors.

CONTACT

Levens
LA8 8PN
015395 60004

Fish & Chips

Crisp, crunchy beer batter encasing delicate, moist white fish, served with a generous helping of thickly cut chips and a side of crushed peas – fish and chips is one of Britain's best comfort foods and is believed to date back over 150 years.

The white fish is typically cod or haddock, served up in cosy pubs or as a take-away traditionally wrapped in paper.

10 of the best

1. *Millers Fish & Chips, Haxby,*
2. *Fylde Fish Bar, Southport*
3. *The Golden Carp Chippy, Redditch*
4. *Burton Road Chippy, Lincoln*
5. *Henley's of Wivenhoe, Wivenhoe*
6. *Captain's Fish and Chips, Hoddesdon*
7. *Harbourside Fish & Chips, Plymouth*
8. *The Magpie, Whitby*
9. *The Golden Galleon, Aldeburgh*
10. *Godfrey's, Harpenden*

Kirkby Lonsdale Brewery

PUB | KIRKBY | LA6 2AB

Kirkby Lonsdale Brewery Co Ltd was established in 2009. Brewing has been at the heart of the town for centuries until the trade had all but died out. The company owners' passion for real ale led to the re-establishment of a local brewery and their pub called The Royal Barn. Situated at the Old Station Yard, the brewery has opened its own beer barn in Kirkby Lonsdale.

The first beer produced by Kirkby Lonsdale Brewery is "Ruskins," named after the iconic Ruskin's View, which Turner famously painted in 1816. The brewery pump clips are branded with an image of local landmark, Devils Bridge and all of their beer names are linked to the local area.

CONTACT

New Road
LA6 2AB
015242 71918

The Bitter End

PUB | COCKERMOUTH | CA13 9PJ

The Bitter End is a traditional pub and restaurant in Cockermouth which is popular with the locals and often busy. Well positioned in this market town, the pub serves a classic menu and changes their specials weekly. Home to one of the smallest breweries in Cumbria, the pub has a good range of real ales and beers alongside wines and an extensive gin menu.

The interior of The Bitter End pub is also traditional with a brick fireplace and woodburner, stone, wood and carpeted floors, a dark wooden bar and comfortable furnishings. This is a dog friendly pub and food here is considered good value.

CONTACT

15 Kirkgate
CA13 9PJ
01900 828993

The Cavendish Arms

PUB | CARTMEL | LA11 6QA

This 450 year old coaching inn is situated in the picturesque village of Cartmel. The Cavendish Arms offers character and charm with a roaring fire and original oak beams. There is a classic pub menu using some local produce with dishes including fish pie and mixed platters for sharing.

Offering stunning views of the South Lakeland District fells and countryside, Cartmel has developed around its 12th Century medieval Priory Church and The Cavendish Arms is at its heart. This medieval village is surrounded by stunning landscape that meets with the sands of Morecambe Bay on the edge of the Furness Peninsula.

CONTACT
Cavendish Street
LA11 6QA
015395 36240

The Dalesman Inn

PUB | SEDBERGH | LA10 5BN

The Dalesman Inn is a fully refurbished, contemporary Free House. With an emphasis on quality, the restaurant menu changes with the seasons and the food is locally sourced. A great base for the Lakes and the Dales, the Dalesman is in the heart of walking country and their homemade ice cream is a welcome treat in the warmer months.

This family-run inn is proud to source its key ingredients locally, with their lamb coming from Hebblethwaite, less than two miles away. The pub is a great place to end up after a riverside walk, with their woodburner and characterful stone walls creating a cozy atmosphere.

CONTACT

Main Street
LA10 5BN
015396 21183

The Fish Pie

A mouthful of maritime delight, the fish pie is a proudly rustic dish that is as filling as it is flavoursome. Clouds of buttery mashed potato and melted cheddar top an unctuous filling of fish and seafood, with smoked haddock, salmon and prawns favourite ingredients.

While the dish is now humbly presented, its roots stem from a 900-year-old royal tradition.

The Factory Tap

PUB | **KENDAL** | LA9 7DE

The Factory Tap claims to be Kendal's premier real ale pub and a location for discovering new hand-crafted beers. Genuine hospitality is key to their ethos and they also carry a selection of quality wines. Pro-active at hosting live music sessions and supporting local art festivals, the pub is at the heart of the community.

The Factory Tap is a contemporary pub set within an old stone building. At the end of each month they bring the culinary delights of street food to the pub and have showcased local foodies' creations; from burgers, fish and chips and Caribbean to Thai, pizzas and vegan friendly offerings.

CONTACT

5 Aynam Road
LA9 7DE
015394 82541

The Highwayman

PUB | KIRKBY LONSDALE | LA6 2RJ

The Highwayman is celebrated for its culinary excellence. The garden terrace is a beautiful spot for al fresco dining during the Summer, whilst glowing log fires inside make it a cozy destination during the Winter. The Highwayman is considered an iconic gastro haven for all seasons.

The Pheasant

PUB | COCKERMOUTH | CA13 9YE

The Pheasant in Bassenthwaite is stylistically stuck in a bit of a time warp but the quality of food and service remains popular today. Using a number of local ingredients in their dishes, you can choose to eat in the slightly more formal Fell Restaurant or in the relaxed bistro.

The Plough

PUB | LUPTON | LA6 1PJ

The Plough near Kirkby Lonsdale is a tastefully styled, contemporary restaurant and hotel situated inside a characterful old coaching inn. With beautiful original beams set against freshly painted walls and a neutral colour palette, the quality and attention to detail offers a little luxury in the countryside.

The Punch Bowl

PUB | LYTH VALLEY | LA8 8HR

The Punch Bowl is situated in the heart of the unspoilt Lyth Valley at Crosthwaite in Cumbria. Offering a 'unique blend of old and new,' The Punch Bowl is a luxurious country restaurant offering quality dining and stylish accommodation. Flickering fires, oak beams and polished oak floors only enhance the ambience.

The Strickland Arms

PUB | KENDAL | LA8 8DZ

Located on the edge of the Lake District, overlooking the entrance to historic Sizergh Castle near Kendal, lies the pub The Strickland Arms. Its interior incorporates light to inky green walls and traditional portraiture and paintings wth an equestrian theme, worn wooden and stone floors with large rugs and grand fireplaces with roaring fires.

The Sun Inn

PUB | KIRKBY LONSDALE | LA6 2AU

The Sun Inn in Kirkby Lonsdale is a 17th century inn well known for its fine, seasonal menu and wine tastings. It combines tradition and charm with modern and stylish design. In a fantastic location where three counties meet, it is within easy access of the Dales, the Lakes and the Trough of Bowland.

The Waterhead

PUB | AMBLESIDE | LA22 0ER

The Waterhead Hotel is yet another fantastic business situated in this beautiful area of the Lake District. Its rustic stone exterior sits amongst immaculate gardens and rolling hills and its riverside location is unbeatable.

Wateredge Inn

PUB | AMBLESIDE | LA22 0EP

The Wateredge Inn has an enviable location right on the shores of beautiful Lake Windermere. Its mesmerising setting offers those wanting to drink or dine, the perfect view, with boats and water steamers cruising by. Wildlife is abundant too and can often be seen from this spectacular spot.

THE CAFE

CAFÉS & TEA ROOMS

LAKE DISTRICT

Baldry's

CAFÉS & TEA ROOMS | AMBLESIDE | LA22 9SP

Baldry's is a vintage style tearoom located in the heart of Grasmere village and renowned for over 25 years for their home baking. Serving light lunches, loose leaf teas, fresh ground coffee and an array of mouth-watering home baked-cakes, this tearoom offers a refined environment.

Baldry's is not like your typical chintzy vintage tearoom, this establishment offers a simple but distinguished interior with large brass mirrors, chandeliers and a solid wood floor. Afternoon tea is served here and is popular. Ingredients used in their home-cooked food are locally sourced from reputable suppliers.

CONTACT

Red Lion Square, Grasmere
LA22 9SP
07760 773671

Bici Café

CAFÉS & TEA ROOMS | ULVERSTON | LA12 7BJ

Bici Café is a modern, authentic Italian café and Kitchen in Ulverston. With an industrial style, the café offers a daytime selection of brunch-style light bites and artisan baked savouries, whilst the evenings are all about their delicious wood-fired pizzas, Italian small plates, salami, cheese and a selection of Italian desserts.

Simplicity and quality are part of the success of Bici Café. With a menu of both traditional and contemporary pizzas, the dough is made using a "long-fermentation" method, adding to the taste and digestability. The ambience is buzzy and relaxed.

CONTACT

1 The Gill
LA12 7BJ
01229 581833

Byre Tea Room

CAFÉS & TEA ROOMS | MILLOM | LA19 5TJ

The Byre Tea Room in Bootle may often be overlooked due to its rather unattractive exterior but inside the barn beams and woodburner create a comfortable stop off in this beautiful area. The food is simple but hugely popular and their sweet afternoon tea platters are beautifully presented and generous.

The relaxed farm table style at the Byre Tea Room makes it a popular choice with families. Dishes are homemade, with lots of local ingredients used within everything from their roasts to their soups. There is also a farm and craft shop on site. With views over the fells, this is a great spot for casual eating.

CONTACT

Millstones Barn, Bootle
LA19 5TJ
01229 718757

Chesters by the River

CAFÉS & TEA ROOMS | AMBLESIDE | LA22 9NJ

Chesters by the River is situated in an enviable position with a deck overlooking the River Brathay. With a counter brimming with some of the finest looking cakes and brownies we ever did see, this contemporary restaurant offers rainbow salads and pizzas and flatbreads from its wood fired oven.

While the counter is covered with some quick to order dishes like frittatas and sausage rolls. The combination of its riverside position and delicious food makes this a popular choice in Ambleside. Sit on the deck to eat and listen to the water cascading past, as the rays of the sun stream through the trees.

CONTACT

Skelwith Bridge
LA22 9NJ
015394 34711

Derwent Isle, Lake District

BY MIKE SMITH

Copper Pot

CAFÉS & TEA ROOMS | AMBLESIDE | LA22 0BU

The Copper Pot café is family owned and one of the most popular in Ambleside. The interior showcases beautiful local materials, from the slate floors to the stone interior walls. With an indulgent array of sumptuous cakes overspilling onto the wooden counter, the quality of food and attention to detail is becoming locally renowned.

The terrace at The Coffee Pot is the perfect spot for coffee or al fresco dining. Inside, a cozy fireplace makes for an idyllic place to sit after a walk on colder days. From homemade burgers and ciabattas to salad plates, the menu is dynamic and places an emphasis on quality.

CONTACT
Church Street
LA22 0BU
015394 31911

Emma's Dell

CAFÉS & TEA ROOMS | AMBLESIDE | LA22 9SX

Emma's Dell is a family owned Crêperie in Grasmere, in the heart of the Lake District. Serving sweet and savoury crepes, homemade cakes, ice cream, artisan coffee, loose leaf-teas and alcohol, this light and airy Crêperie is contemporary in style.

Emma's Dell was inspired by a ski trip taken by Emma and her family and their love of their apres ski indulgences. Sumptuous and indulgent cakes in glass stands line the counter here, whilst a delicious array of homemade ice creams can be selected from the chalkboard menu. Ice creams range from Madagascan Vanilla and Gingerbread to vegan Coconut.

CONTACT

Grasmere
LA22 9SX
015394 35234

Farrer's of Kendal

CAFÉS & TEA ROOMS | KENDAL | LA9 4LY

Farrer's is a traditional tea and coffee house with an old-fashioned sleek black exterior, bay windows and gold signage. Inside, it has the feel of an old apothecary with enormous tins of a vast array of tea and coffee varieties, sold by helpful and informative staff.

Enjoy many of Farrer's special varieties of tea and coffee in their café area with its glowing woodburner and old portraiture on the walls. Soups, sandwiches, pastries and traditional dishes are served in this simple, specialist store. If you don't want to stop, takeaway drinks are also available.

CONTACT

13 Stricklandgate
LA9 4LY
015397 31707

Fellpack

CAFÉS & TEA ROOMS | **KESWICK** | **CA12 5BS**

Fellpack is 'the unique creation of a group of friends with a thirst for adventure and a love of great food'. Their ethos is to create delicious food from local ingredients whilst enjoyed in the comfort of their restaurant or taken away to enjoy in front of breathtaking views from a fell top, or one of the many beautiful lakes.

Fellpack's considered menu balances 'classic flavours with bold innovation.' Dishes are generally healthy and creative. The restaurant has a stylish and rustic aesthetic and serves delicious coffee alongside flapjacks and brownies, for those needing some extra hiking fuel.

CONTACT

19 Lake Road
CA12 5BS
017687 71177

Wasdale, Lake District

BY NEIL MANNING

Gillam's Tea Room & Grocer

CAFÉS & TEA ROOMS | ULVERSTON | LA12 7LT

Gillam's Tea Room and Specialist grocer is an institution in Ulverston, with the Gillam family having provided fine food and excellent service in Ulverston since 1892, when John James Gillam opened his cash and wholesale grocers on Market Street. Today the tearoom offers wholesome home-cooked food made from local produce and the grocery sells organic fruit and vegetables, with an emphasis on provenance.

Gillam's has retained many of the store's original features and old-world charm; from its fireplace, high ceilings and tea-lined shelves to the quality of service and pretty store front.

CONTACT
64 Market Street
LA12 7LT
01229 587564

Grange Café

CAFÉS & TEA ROOMS | BORROWDALE | CA12 5XA

Grange Café is wonderfully located in the village of Grange, near the River Derwent where the 1675 double-arched bridge still impresses visitors. The café offers light lunches and sweet treats and has seating both inside and out where you can marvel at the mountains rising high above you on both sides.

The surrounding area is filled with fantastic walks and this makes Grange Café the perfect spot for refreshment. On a cold day you can enjoy local spiced sticky toffee pudding with custard and in the summer nothing beats quality cream tea.

CONTACT

Grange View
CA12 5XA
017687 77077

Lanercost Tea Room & Gift Shop

CAFÉS & TEA ROOMS | **LANERCOST** | CA8 2HQ

Lanercost Tea Room specialises in fresh, homemade food using quality local produce. The tea room is situated next door to the 12th century Lanercost Priory and a short walk from the World Heritage site of Hadrian's Wall. The wall dates back to 128 AD when it served as a defensive fortification in the Roman province of Britannia under the reign of emperor Hadrian.

There is also a gift shop on site selling locally made products including pure wool throws and decor items for the home. If you are looking to explore Hadrian's Wall then this makes an ideal starting point. Parking is free and dogs are welcome too.

CONTACT
Brampton
CA8 2HQ
016977 41267

Langwathby Station Café

CAFÉS & TEA ROOMS | LANGWATHBY | CA10 1NB

Langwathby is an attractive and remote train station on the famous Settle to Carlisle line and set within the old waiting room is this intimate little café. Popular with cyclists and walkers who come for their famous cherry scone with cream and jam and home made quiche. Service is friendly and prices are reasonable.

Take shelter from those wet and windy days and warm up in front of their open fire. You might even be lucky enough to see the Flying Scotsman steam engine pass through on its way north. Dogs are welcome.

CONTACT
Langwathby
CA10 1NB
01768 881151

Rufford Old Hall

LANCASHIRE

Lingholm Kitchen

CAFÉS & TEA ROOMS | KESWICK | CA12 5TZ

The octagonal walled garden sits on the same spot as the old Lingholm Kitchen gardens which Beatrix Potter credited as her inspiration for Mr McGregor's garden in The Tale of Peter Rabbit. Built in a Victorian style, the garden has herbaceous borders while central areas are reserved for vegetables which are then served fresh in the Kitchen.

Lingholm Kitchen aims to offer the best day time eating experience in the area. Its emphasis on food provenance can be seen on their boards, where they list the farms and suppliers of their local meat and dairy produce. Local and seasonal ingredients are a focus.

CONTACT

Lingholm Lodge
CA12 5TZ
017687 71206

Lunesdale Bakery

CAFÉS & TEA ROOMS | KIRKBY LONSDALE | LA6 2AJ

This long-established, traditional bakery and tearoom has maintained its reputation over the years for its quality artisanal breads, pastries, cakes and savoury produce. The charm here is in its reputation and emphasis on its produce.

Next door to the bakery is their tearoom with a roaring fire and old-fashioned cozy ambience. Serving traditional food, the tearoom serves breakfasts and lunches in generous portions. Step back in time with a slower pace and style here at Kirkby Lonsdale's Lunesdale Bakery and Tearoom.

CONTACT
50 Main Street
LA6 2AJ
015242 71296

Merienda

CAFÉS & TEA ROOMS | KESWICK | CA12 5JD

Merienda is an exceptionally stylish and contemporary licensed restaurant/café serving breakfast and brunch through to an eclectic evening menu. With a simple, globally influenced menu, the founders' aim has been to use wholesome, seasonal ingredients whilst drawing inspiration from around the world.

Exceptional ingredients are the focus at Merienda and they are serious about their coffee too, serving the delicious Monmouth brand. This is a sleek establishment with sophisticated design, from its light parquet flooring and creative pendant lighting to its artistic installation above the beautifully crafted bar.

CONTACT
10 Main Street
CA12 5JD
017687 72024

Mr H Tearoom

CAFÉS & TEA ROOMS | AMBLESIDE | LA22 0AD

Mr H's in Ambleside is a light and airy café with high ceilings, large windows and plenty of natural light. Serving teas, coffees, cakes and sandwiches, this is a casual spot with lovely views of the town. Cake stands with tiers of scones and home-baked indulgences are placed on the counter.

With vintage accessories and details highlighting the walls and shelves, the staff are friendly and the presentation is good. Conveniently located near to the bus stop, Mr H's Tearoom offers simple, tasty dishes in the heart of the town.

CONTACT

Lake Road
LA22 0AD
015394 31421

Carnforth Railway Station

LANCASHIRE

No. 6 Finkle Street

CAFÉS & TEA ROOMS | SEDBERGH | LA10 5BZ

No. 6 Finkle Street in Sedburgh has everything you need in terms of home décor. Lighting, kitchen and dining accessories, linens, bedding and a huge range of gifts make this a great browsing and shopping experience. They also operate the Mad Hatters Tea Room where cakes and light lunches can be enjoyed.

You can buy all of their lifestyle stock on their website online. However, to get a real feel for the products, a visit to their shop is best. After stocking up on decorative items for your home, you can treat yourself to afternoon tea at Mad Hatters.

CONTACT
6 Finkle Street
LA10 5BZ
015396 20298

Poppi Red

CAFÉS & TEA ROOMS | HAWKSHEAD | LA22 0NT

Poppi Red in Hawkshead is a warm and welcoming café and gift shop selling a delicious range of cakes and pastries, freshly ground coffee and big pots of tea. This is the dream of the owner Kim, who spent many years travelling, only to come back and miss the beautiful shops that she had visited on her journeys. She decided to create her own here in Hawkshead.

Uplifting quotes feature on the walls and floral prints, polka dots and stripes in candy colour tones create a breezy, feminine aesthetic. Poppi Red is licensed and sells the locally brewed Hawkshead lager and a local damson gin in the summer months.

CONTACT

Main Street
LA22 0NT
015394 36434

Rattle Gill Café

CAFÉS | AMBLESIDE | LA22 9DU

The Rattle Gill Café provides hearty, home cooked goodness in the beautiful surroundings of Ambleside. Baking fresh cakes each day, they also offer their famous Cake Platter; 5 different slices of cake for sweet enthusiasts. The menu offers extensive vegetarian options from homemade soups and veggie chilli to baked potatoes and toated sandwiches.

Rogan & Company

CAFÉS | CARTMEL | LA11 6QD

Rogan & Company is the sister restaurant to Simon Rogan's nationally acclaimed L'Enclume. Rogan & Co offers a more casual dining experience while "retaining the unparalleled precision and creativity of Simon's distinctive culinary style, using exceptional Cumbrian, as well as home-grown, ingredients that are harvested in their prime."

Sarah's

CAFÉS | COCKERMOUTH | CA13 9LU

Sarah's in Cockermouth is a simply furnished, contemporary craft café offering high quality teas and coffees alongside a selection of home-baked scones, cakes and light lunches. Service is warm and friendly and the atmosphere is relaxed.

Syke Farm Tearoom

CAFÉS | BUTTERMERE | CA13 9XA

Syke Farm Tea Room is a rustic, farmhouse style café. The farm specialises in Ayrshire dairy cows which means that some of the freshest, regionally renowned ice cream is made and served here. This is the perfect indulgence after a walk around the hypnotically beautiful Buttermere Lake.

The Bakery at No.4

CAFÉS | KENDAL | LA9 4QB

Based in Kendal, The Bakery at No.4 specialises in making beautiful bespoke wedding cakes, as well as celebration cakes and classic afternoon teas. Only top quality ingredients including free range eggs, real butter and local ales are used in their delicious, high quality creations.

The Crossing Point Café

CAFÉS | KIRKBY LONSDALE | LA6 2AN

Owned and managed by John and Renata Strange, The Crossing Point Café is "the culmination of a dream – an eatery that is all about local produce, the freshest food". Wholesome, home-cooked food is created by the team from carefully selected seasonal ingredients, to ensure exceptional flavour and provenance.

The Hazelmere

CAFÉS | GRANGE-OVER-SANDS | LA11 6ED

The Hazelmere is an independent, family-run café and delicatessen in Grange-over-Sands. Community and environment are hugely important to The Hazelmere and they invest in both by supporting local suppliers and by making and baking on site.

The Jumble Room

CAFÉS | GRASMERE | LA22 9SU

The Jumble Room is a vibrant and intimate restaurant established over twenty years ago by the owners Andy and Chrissy who are passionate about food. The menu focuses on local and organic produce with Thai and Mediterranean accents. The food has gained a reputation for its excellence and the service is rather exceptional too.

The Moon & Sixpence

CAFÉS | COCKERMOUTH | CA13 9LE

The Moon and Sixpence is an artisanal coffee shop in Cockermouth which has built a strong reputation for its high quality coffee and home-baked pastries. The owner, Stephen Kidd, has immersed himself in coffee culture and even lived in one of the world's coffee capitals, Vancouver where he gleaned experience from the experts.

The Moon Highgate

CAFÉS | KENDAL | LA9 4EN

The Moon Highgate in Kendal is a restaurant offering 'expertly prepared, high quality food in a comfortable, relaxed setting'. Head Chef and proprietor Leon Whitehead has created a contemporary British menu that changes with the seasons and is carefully crafted to make the most of the finest local ingredients.

The Pig

CAFÉS | WINDERMERE | LA23 1EA

The Pig in Windermere is a contemporary restaurant offering a classic British menu based on fresh local produce. Pork in all its forms is their specialty. From juicy ribs and their popular pig platter to smoked pig and a hog roast, which is cooked daily on the rotisserie, The Pig is a carnivore's paradise.

The Square Orange Café

CAFÉS | KESWICK | CA12 5AS

The Square Orange offers true continental café culture with a speciality coffee menu. The bar serves a selection of local and continental beers and wines and their specialities are their fresh coffee and authentic Stonebaked Pizza.

The Windmill Café

CAFÉS | CALDBECK | CA7 8DR

The Watermill Café in Caldbeck specialises in delicious home-cooked food using only the finest local produce, served in the beautiful surroundings of a converted watermill. In warmer weather sit on the terrace with views over the river Caldbeck. During the winter months the restaurant is warmed by a cosy log stove and lit by candles.

The Yard Kitchen

CAFÉS | PENRITH | CA11 7LU

The Yard Kitchen is a bright and open, cute little café, which is located at Penrith's Brunswick Yard. White brick walls line the interior where pressed flowers are displayed in frames. There is also a stove, which runs through the cooler months, warming customers alongside hot drinks, such as artisan coffee, hot chocolate and tea.

Three Hares

CAFÉS | SEDBURGH | LA10 5AB

The Three Hares is a family run seasonal and locally sourced café, bistro and bakery situated in the book town of Sedbergh at the foot of the Howgills. The cooking style here is influenced by the founders heritage of both the wild food of the local area and growing up in Germany with Japanese parents.

Waterhead Coffee

CAFÉS | AMBLESIDE | LA22 0EY

With mesmerising views of the lake, Waterhead Coffee in Ambleside offers one of the most scenic spots in the lakes for a coffee and something home-baked. Beautifully presented cakes are placed on slate boards and a pretty outside window on the terrace serves ice creams on warmer days.

BEST OF ENGLAND

FOOD
SHOPS

LAKE DISTRICT

Cartmel Cheeses and Bakery

FOOD SHOPS | CARTMEL | LA11 6PN

Cartmel Cheeses & Bakery is one of the delightful businesses nestled within Unsworth's Yard. Unsurprisingly given its name, the shop specialises in a wide range of British, Irish and French cheeses and freshly baked goods. It makes an ideal stop to gather a few picnic nibbles for a day out exploring the Lake District.

The village of Cartmel has become a a popular culinary destination, best known for its Michelin starred L'Enclume restaurant and this shop holds its own amongst such prestigious company. Be sure to pop in to Unsworth's Yard Brewery next door for a tasting before you head out into the countryside.

CONTACT
Grange Over Sands
LA11 6PN
015395 34307

![Dales Traditional Butchers storefront]

Dales Traditional Butchers

FOOD SHOPS | **KIRKBY LONSDALE** | LA6 2AU

Dales Traditional Butchers have been supplying quality, locally reared meats for over 100 years in Kirkby Lonsdale. Established in 1906 by Herbert Dale, the produce comes from local farms who supply only the highest quality meats from Cumbrian and Lancastrian land.

The produce ranges from traditional meats, pies and puddings to fine cheeses and fresh vegetables at Dales Traditional Butchers. Staff are friendly and experienced and their award winning pies are all produced in house to traditional recipes, using only the best locally sourced ingredients.

CONTACT
2 Market Street
LA6 2AU
015242 71278

Grasmere Gingerbread Shop

FOOD SHOPS | GRASMERE | LA22 9SW

The Grasmere Gingerbread Shop was established by Victorian cook Sarah Nelson in 1854. The reputation of her delicious gingerbread quickly gained traction and today the shop's famous clientele includes Hollywood actor Tom Cruise. This tiny shop was Sarah Nelson's Church Cottage home and remains almost untouched to this day.

Sarah Nelson's original gingerbread recipe is hand-written on parchment and safely stored away in a secure bank safe in the Lake District. The only person alive today who knows the recipe is Andrew Hunter, a partner in the business, who mixes and bakes the gingerbread fresh every day.

CONTACT

Church Cottage
LA22 9SW
015394 35428

Kitridding Farm Shop

FOOD SHOPS | KIRKBY LONSDALE | LA6 2QA

Kitridding Farm Shop is an award-winning family business selling farm-to-table, native breed, traditionally butchered meats from their farm shop in Kirkby Lonsdale. All their animals are traditionally home reared without intensive, industrial farming methods. Their animals graze in fields between Spring and late Autumn and are housed during the winter months and fed on grass harvested in the summer.

The provenance of their produce is something Kitridding Farm Shop feel passionately about. Humane practices are part of their ethos and ensured at every stage of production including within their family-run abattoir.

CONTACT

Kitridding
LA6 2QA
01539 567484

Low Howgill Butchers & Deli

FOOD SHOPS | **KESWICK** | **CA12 5DQ**

Low Howgil Butchers & Deli is an award-winning destination food shop serving high quality meats, pies and delicatessen produce. With an on-site bakery, the shop offers some of the freshest pies around, always incorporating their own meat into the recipes. Their traditional meats and associated produce often have a seasonal twist.

The meat here at Low Howgil Butchers and Deli comes from the family farm and ingredients are from local farms wherever possible. The farm to fork ethos has made the shop a popular choice in the region. The interior is contemporary and the branding is stylish.

CONTACT

34 Lake Road
CA12 5DQ
017687 72666

Lake Windermere

CUMBRIA

Low Sizergh Barn

FOOD SHOPS | **KENDAL** | **LA8 8AE**

Records show a farm has existed on the site of Low Sizergh Barn since the 13th century. Once the home farm of Sizergh Castle, the farm today is one of the largest providers of dairy produce in the region. The welfare of the animals and the natural environment is of paramount importance to the farm.

Alongside a beautiful 17th century barn farm shop offering quality produce with provenance, the café above the milking sheds offers cooked breakfasts, light lunches and farmhouse teas. Every afternoon around 3.30pm the farm's cows come in to be milked and the café's large windows provide the perfect viewing gallery.

CONTACT

Low Sizergh Barn
LA8 8AE
01539 560426

Plumgarths Farm Shop

FOOD SHOPS | KENDAL | LA8 8LX

Plumgarths Farm Shop offers a one-stop shop for the best local farm produce. From meat, dressings, preserves, ice-creams, ales, breads, baked goods, fruit and vegetables, all items stocked are from local and passionate small-scale producers.

Next door to Plumgarths Farm Shop is the popular Two Sisters Café, serving hearty breakfasts, light lunches and opulent afternoon teas. The sister team are passionate about baking and creating a welcoming environment to enjoy their home-cooked food. The café is simple in style with lots of light and a woodburner for colder days.

CONTACT

Crook Road
LA8 8LX
01539 736300

Lake Windermere

Relish

FOOD SHOPS | HAWKSHEAD | LA22 0NZ

The Hawkshead Relish Company is an artisan producer of award-winning preserves. The range of over 120 relishes, pickles and preserves are handmade in small batches, using traditional open pans and locally sourced ingredients.

Staff of Life

FOOD SHOPS | KENDAL | LA9 4AB

Staff of Life is a family-run artisan bakery in Kendal. Hand-made bread is offered fresh every day and customers enjoy purchasing the bread often straight from the oven. Breads are mixed the night before and left to slowly rise using little yeast or salt. They also pride themselves on their sourdoughs which use local damson and elderflower ingredients.

The Little Ice Cream Shop

FOOD SHOPS | HAWKSHEAD | LA22 0NZ

The Little Ice Cream Shop is Hawkshead's first specialist artisan ice cream shop. Serving 22 delicious and unique flavours of pure indulgence, their ice cream is made by a local farm who have been making luxurious ice cream from their small dairy herd since 1948.

Tony Harrison

FOOD SHOPS | COCKERMOUTH | CA13 9LU

Tony Harrison is a butchers in Cockermouth and provides native breed, free range, pasture fed, dry aged meat carefully selected from small farmers who care. Their meat is seasonal and they source directly from the farms, ensuring that the meat is fully traceable and of a high quality.

BEST OF ENGLAND

CULTURE & HISTORY

LAKE DISTRICT

Abbot Hall Art Gallery

CULTURE | KENDAL | LA9 5AL

Abbot Hall Art Gallery is a Grade I listed museum and gallery that was built in 1759 by Colonel George Wilson, whose family owned a large house and country estate nearby. The gallery showcases contemporary and historic art including portraits by 18th-century local artist George Romney as well as 300 years of British landscape paintings.

The building was rescued by locals having fallen into disrepair in the 1950s and recently won the Art Gallery of the Year Cumbria Life Culture Awards. The gallery is located beside the river in the heart of the Cumbrian town of Kendal.

CONTACT

Kirkland
LA9 5AL
01539 722464

Blackwell, The Arts & Crafts House

CULTURE | BOWNESS | LA23 3JT

Blackwell, The Arts & Crafts House was completed in 1900 and is an outstanding example of British architecture. The large house overlooks Lake Windermere and is full of rare impressive features, including hessian wall hangings, carved wooden paneling and stained glass windows.

The gardens are laid out as a series of terraces and offer fantastic views and the flowerbeds and long sweeping lawn enhance this stunning location. The shop on-site has plenty of gifts for those after something special to take home and regular exhibitions add to the displays and sit well with the impressive furnishings.

CONTACT

Bowness-on-Windermere
LA23 3JT
01539 446139

Holmes Mill

CULTURE | CLITHEROE | BB7 1EB

Based in the heart of Clitheroe, Holmes Mill is a unique celebration of Lancashire food, drink and entertainment. This former textiles mill provides an impressive industrial interior and plays host to a beer hall, a stylish hotel, a popular grill restaurant and a vibrant food hall.

The Bowland Food Hall showcases the very best of Lancashire's food and drink producers. This modern temple of gastronomic indulgence provides a platform for local, passionate food and drink producers across the northwest, to bring the finest fare to your plate. Most of them are small independent artisan producers who farm or grow in Lancashire.

CONTACT
Greenacre Street
BB7 1EB
01200 407120

![Brough Castle on a ridge with sheep grazing on the grassy slope below](image)

Brough Castle

CULTURE | BROUGH | CA17 4EJ

Standing on a ridge along the Stanmore Pass is the impressive remains of Brough Castle beside the river Swindale Beck. The castle was built on the site of a Roman fort and its towering keep dates from about 1200. It was an easy target for the Scots and was raided frequently.

The Clifford Family extended its living quarters on the site shortly after 1510 and when celebrating Christmas with a great party in 1521 they were accidently burned down. In the 17th century, Lady Ann Clifford restored much of the castle and you can still see much of this restoration today. A walk around Brough Castle is pleasant and interesting.

CONTACT

Rosemount
CA17 4EJ
0370 3331181

Old Bark Mill

AMBLESIDE, CUMBRIA

Carlisle Cathedral

CULTURE | CARLISLE | CA3 8TZ

A visit to Carlisle Cathedral is surely memorable. The ceiling glistens with gold and the ancient medieval choir stalls have withstood time and are worth running your hand along the smooth surfaces. It's gone through a series of building phases and has just been awarded a grant to re-build the dining hall known as the Frantry building.

A church has stood here for around 900 years and there are plenty of features to take you on an historic journey. To gain an even better in-depth knowledge of the nooks and crannies you can take a tour of the Cathedral. Evensong is sung daily in the church and there is also a daily service.

CONTACT

7 Abbey Street
CA3 8TZ
01228 548151

Cathedral Cavern

CULTURE | AMBLESIDE | LA22 9PB

Cathedral Cavern, an explorer's dream, is a network of old slate quarries, located just above the Little Langdale Valley. The highlight of the quarry is the grand main chamber. It reaches up over 40 foot high and has two large openings that let in generous amounts of natural light so that you can see quite easily the pool of water and central column.

To reach Cathedral Cavern is relatively straightforward, however, be sure to take a torch for the tunnels and wear sturdy boots, as the paths are often slippery and wet. A visit is exciting for all ages and the acoustics are unique in the main cavern, so sing your heart out.

CONTACT

LA22 9PB

Derwent Pencil Museum

CULTURE | KESWICK | CA12 5NG

After the discovery of graphite in the Barrowdale Valley the birth of the pencil was imminent. The Cumberland Pencil Company created its first pencil in Keswick in 1832 and the first factory was built the same year. The Derwent Pencil Museum is located beside the old factory and tells the story of the interesting journey the company has been through.

Highlights include a replica graphite mine, secret WW2 pencils with hidden maps, one of the largest pencils in the world and miniature pencil sculptures. On site is a large fine art retail shop, where you can purchase all the creative drawing materials you desire.

CONTACT

Southey Works
CA12 5NG
017687 73626

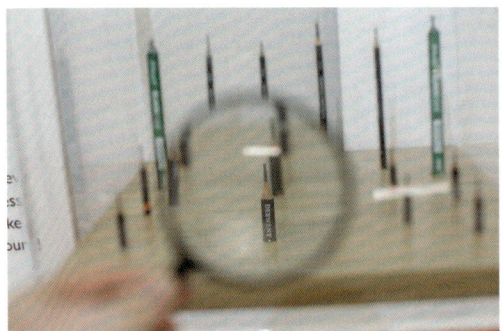

Fairfield Mill

CULTURE | SEDBERGH | LA10 5LW

Fairfield Mill is a Victorian Woollen Mill located in the heart of the Yorkshire Dales. Originally built in 1837, the mill was the last surviving woollen mill in the Western Dales and produced textiles for 156 years. The mill was lovingly restored in 2001 with new life has been breathed in to this charming industrial structure and the rugged stone exterior.

Today, there are four floors of exhibition space showcasing local heritage and textile arts. Step back in time to understand how the mill operated and the products it made. There is also a cafe on site and parking is free.

CONTACT

Garsdale Road
LA10 5LW
015396 21958

St James' Church

BUTTERMERE, CUMBRIA

Heaton Cooper Studio & Gallery

CULTURE | **GRASMERE** | **LA22 9SX**

Established in 1905, the Heaton Cooper Studio is a thriving, family-run art gallery, bookshop, exhibition space and attractive modern café called Mathilde's, which overlooks the village green of Grasmere and out to the hills beyond.

Heaton Cooper Studio is home to the Heaton Cooper family set of artists and it exhibits past and present work from the family tree, including prints and paintings of the beautiful surrounding area. There is also a well-stocked art shop on site with world-class materials, for creatives. If you're visiting Grasmere, then it's well worth a visit.

CONTACT

Broadgate
LA22 9SX
015394 35280

Lakeland Motor Museum

CULTURE | ULVERSTON | LA12 8TA

Lakeland Motor Museum has over 30,000 exhibits from around the world and chronicles the history of motoring through the twentieth century. The museum is a marvellous homage to the internal combustion engine and is housed in a converted mill. On display are cars, motorbikes, pedal cars, bicycles and the occasional unique machine.

The museum also sports numerous motor-related artefacts such as vintage petrol pumps and special collections relating to the Campbell Bluebird and Isle of Man TT display. Many hours can be spent marvelling at the beauty and design of bygone ages, with classics from Europe and the US.

CONTACT

Old Blue Mill, Backbarrow
LA12 8TA
015395 30400

Lancaster Castle

CULTURE | LANCASTER | LA1 1YJ

Lancaster Castle is historically fascinating and dates back to Roman times, when its commanding position on the hill overlooking the town of Lancaster and the River Lune protected the area from invasion. The castle today offers insight into the nation's religious and cultural beliefs throughout the centuries.

Lancaster Castle is open daily for guided tours and visitors can enjoy the courtyard spaces, external views of the historic building, two small exhibition spaces and the giftshop without charge. Public access to the interiors of the castle buildings is by guided tour only.

CONTACT

Castle Park
LA1 1YJ
01524 64998

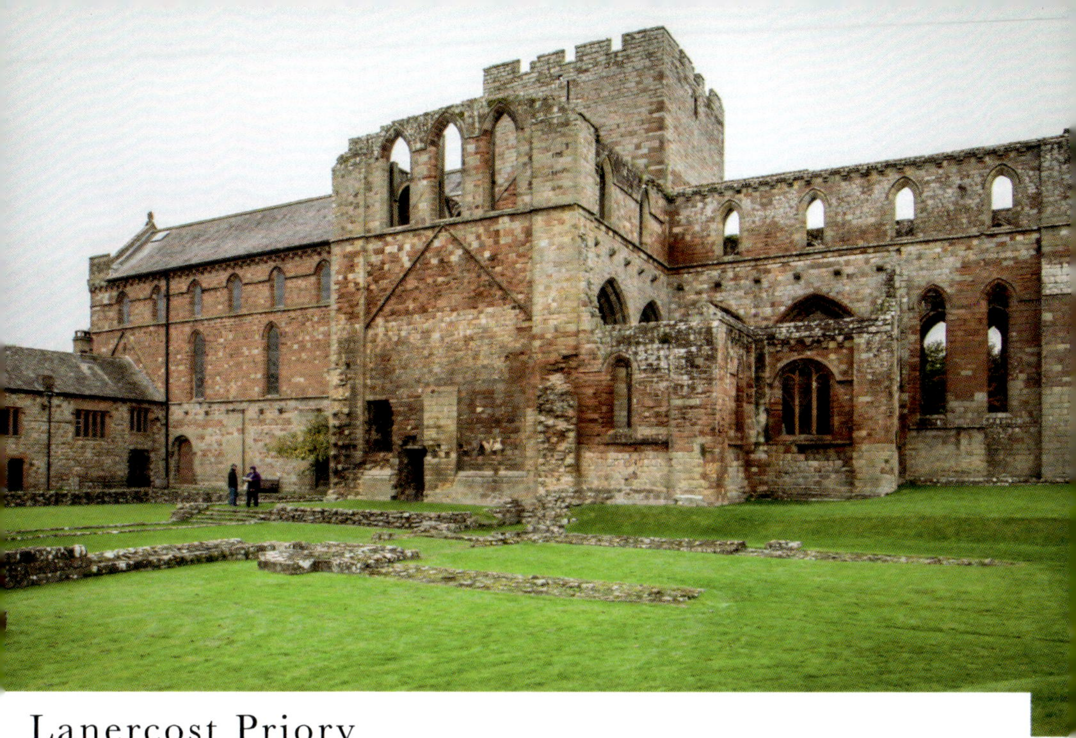

Lanercost Priory

CULTURE | LANERCOST | CA8 2HQ

The best preserved of all Cumbria's priories, Lanercost is a dramatic and impressive edifice. It suffered many attacks over the years from the Scots due to its close proximity to Hadrian's Wall. Considering the frequent attacks, the east end of the noble 13th Century Church survived to its full height and the dramatic triple tiers of arches are still admired by those who visit.

Lanercoast Priory includes a working church, the ruins of the monastic buildings, tombs, Roman stonework and altars. There's a lot to see and do at this English Heritage site and there is a tearoom 100 yards from the Priory, ideal for refreshment.

CONTACT

Near Brampton
CA8 2HQ
01697 73030

Honister Pass

KESWICK, LAKE DISTRICT

Muncaster Castle

CULTURE | **RAVENGLASS** | **CA18 1RQ**

Muncaster Castle is an historic haunted building, surrounded by tranquil Himalayan gardens and bluebell woods. It overlooks the beautiful Eskdale Valley and the river Esk and is a short drive from Ravenglass town, for which it may have acted as a fort in the past. The Pennington family owns the Castle and they have lived at Muncaster for at least 800 years.

Today the site includes a hawk and owl centre, meadow vole maze and adventure playgrounds, a café, gift shop and accommodation. They run exciting events and festivals throughout the year and the castle is often used for ceremonies and functions.

CONTACT
Muncaster
CA18 1RQ
01229 717614

St Lawrence's Church

CULTURE | APPLEBY | CA16 6QN

St Lawrence's Church in Appleby-in-Westmorland is an active Anglican parish church in the deanery of Appleby. The lower part of the tower on St Lawrence's Church dates from about 1150 and the main body originates from the 14th and 15th centuries.

As well as many of her castle estates Lady Anne Clifford restored the church and rebuilt the north chapel. She even designed her own memorial tomb which you can see when visiting. St Lawrence's Church is united with six other local churches that form the benefice of Heart of Eden. It's an impressive building with grand arches and is worth visiting when in Appleby.

CONTACT

Boroughgate
CA16 6QN
017683 61269

Ambleside, Cumbria

BY GEORGE HILES

The Dent Heritage Centre

CULTURE | DENT | LA10 5QJ

Beautifully designed by local labourers, the Dent Heritage Centre provides a wealth of information about the working lives and history of the Dales area. The artefacts and objects have been carefully collected and lovingly restored, providing a fascinating glimpse into days gone by.

The Old Grammar School

CULTURE | HAWKSHEAD | LA22 0NT

The Old Grammar School in Hawkshead is a marvelous historical site in the heart of the Lake District. It was originally founded in 1585 by the Archbishop of York as a school and taught Latin grammar, ancient history and the sciences. It was a unique Tudor school, governed by a charter from Queen Elizabeth I.

The Rum Story

CULTURE | WHITEHAVEN | CA28 7DN

The Rum Story is a museum in Whitehaven set in the original 1785 rum shop and which takes you on an interactive journey through the history of the spirit. They have wonderful themed rooms filled with surprises throughout; the rooms include a rainforest, an African village, a slave ship, and a Coopers workshop.

Theatre by the Lake

CULTURE | KESWICK | CA12 5DJ

Theatre by the Lake is quite possibly the best-located theatre in Britain, a short walk from Derwentwater on the edge of Keswick. It first opened in 1999 and has two stages; the Main House with 400 seats and the Studio with 100 seats. The Theatre present nine of their own productions throughout the year and their Christmas plays are a favourite for the whole family.

Discover what's nearby with our app

Use our app to find out what's nearby and use our
maps to help you get there.

Available for iOS and Android phones.

Find out more at

bestofengland.com/app

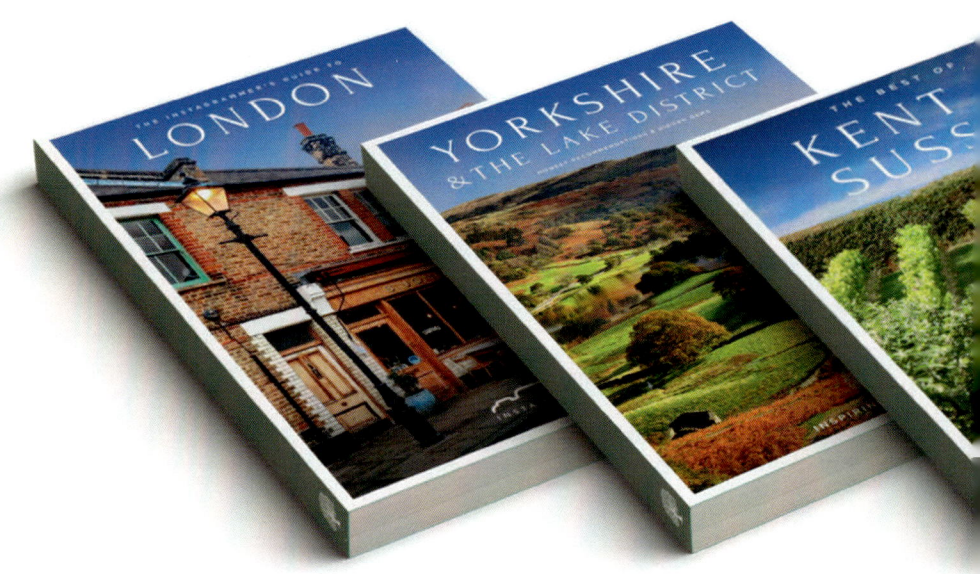

Meet the family

Unique photographic travel guides.

www.bestofengland.shop

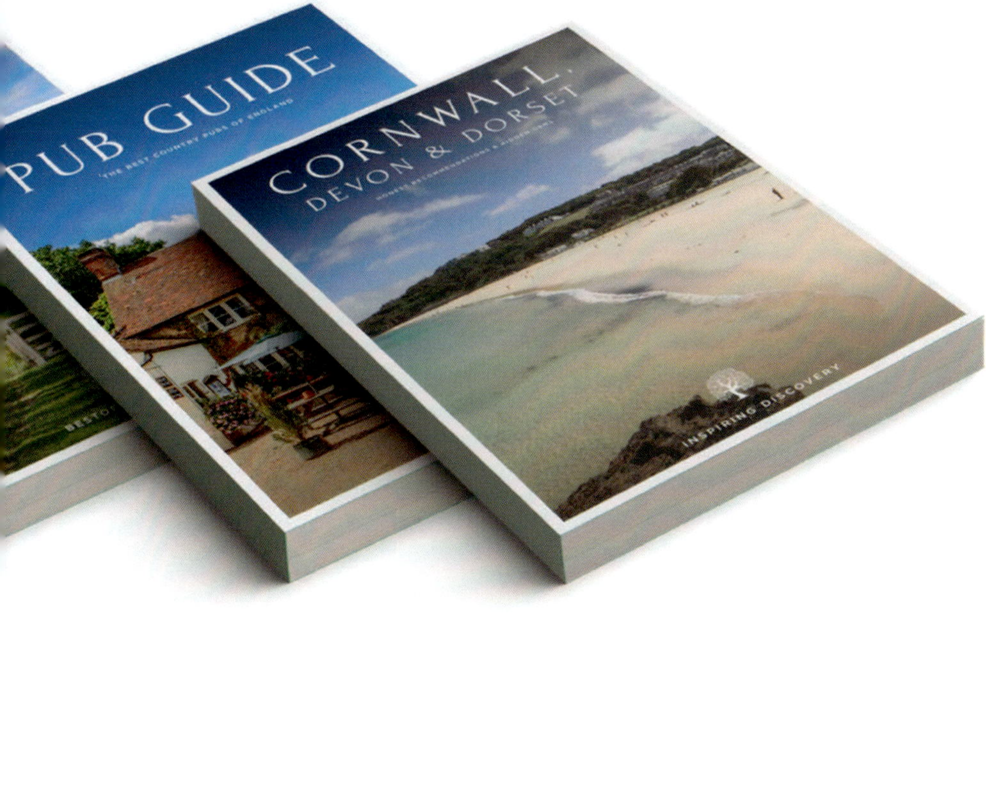

Enjoy 10% off your
next purchase using
the code: **bestoffriends**